To John

Kenn Flemmons

Design by Peggy Farra
Printing by Target Printing
Little Rock, Arkansas, USA

Published by Goldcrest Holdings, LLC
1014 W. Third Street
Little Rock, Arkansas 72201

This book may be purchased from the
author. Contact him at 501-376-2278 or
kflemmons@southernbarter.com

COVER PHOTO:
While there is no definitive explanation of this picture that exists, some
clues are obvious. This appears to be the Brewer's Union members posing
for a photo in front of a parade float, possibly before a Labor Day parade.
With enough magnification, you can see the banner on the back which
has "Brewer's Union" on it. King Gambrinus, the Patron Saint of beer, sits
atop one of the brewery's aging tanks, aided by two helpers in pantaloons.
The age of the photo is late 1890s or early 1900s. The buildings behind
the men were the original brewery buildings, torn down in 1963. The
large building at the far left is still there.

Acknowledgments

No endeavor like writing a history of a company and the people that made it up is easy. Hours are spent pouring through thousands of pieces of paper searching out the details that make up the story. Dozens of people are interviewed and hundreds of records reviewed looking for clues. Some say that it is a labor of love. I can not argue with that but I know I have enjoyed every minute. While this book has now been written, I expect to add to my knowledge about the brewery for years to come.

It was my privilege to have my wife, Mari R. Flemmons, at my side through it all, both as support and as someone to review my manuscript. Her literary training was a great help in polishing my grammar. Syntax has never been my strong point.

Gratitude is also due Tom Bates who helped rescue the history of the brewery years ago and has stored the hundreds of boxes in his attic since. Without Tom saving those boxes full of records, a lot of what you read in this book would not have been known.

I feel very fortunate that I was able to meet and talk to E.C. "Buddy" Krausnick, Jr., the brewery's last president. Mr. "Buddy" was not only a great aid in compiling this book, he was a real treat to interview.

This work would have been incomplete without contributions from many others. Some helped with their memories and others by allowing items from their collections to be photographed. Gene Bradberry, Ed Bretherick, Jack Borg, Ray Brown, Richard Campbell, Bill Carter, Dick Caughey, Charlotte Clark, Marty Coco, Walter Crews, Fred Dettwiller, Doris Dolan, George Eckert, David Ehring, Mary Lou Gaerig, Carolyn Gilmore, Alan Hart, Jane Scott Howell, Bob Kay, Kevin Kious, Katherine Kuehn, Bill Lockhart, Henry and Lynn Loenneke, Jay Marsh, Ruth Meredith, Hal and Ronna Newburger, Kevin Norman, Jack and Kitty Patterson, Ronnie Pevahouse, Ed Provine, Jim and Martha Reardon, Michael Reardon, Don Roussin, Jacob B. "Jake" Schorr, III, Eleanor Scott, Joe Signaigo, Tom Phillips, Jack Tucker and Doug Yancey were most generous in their time and resources.

Special thanks go to Pere Magness whose column in the Memphis Commercial Appeal helped locate several of the people listed in the previous paragraph; Jim Johnson of the history department of the Memphis/Shelby County Public Library and Ed Frank of the University of Memphis library for their research assistance; Claude Jones of the Commercial Appeal for his help in locating several photographs; Lynn Craig for her proofreading help; and the Beer Can Collectors of America for the digital photographs of the Tennessee Brewing Company's cans.

Lastly, I want to thank my good friend the late Vic Olson whose encouragement to tackle the task of telling this story was pivotal. I dedicate this book to his memory.

Chapter One

*I*t was probably not the best time to begin a business in Memphis, Tennessee. The city was only beginning to recover from Reconstruction when a yellow fever epidemic hit in 1878. The primitive medical care of the day was of little help, and more than 5,000 people died, while 25,000 more simply moved away. By the end of the decade, Memphis was bankrupt and only half occupied. As a result, the State of Tennessee revoked Memphis' city charter in 1879 and made it a taxing district of the state. Yet, against this backdrop of gloom many people remained, life went on, business continued, and a new one, the Memphis Brewing Company, opened.

Between the end of the War Between the States and 1877, thirteen breweries operated in Memphis. (1/1) Most opened and closed the same year. A few, like Sebastian Kaufman's City Brewery, stayed in business for more than a year. All the breweries were small, with little going for them except desire. Francis Schulz operated his brewery outside Memphis in Fort Pickering, (1/2) and in 1874 produced 205 barrels of beer. By the following year, that reached 295 barrels. (1/3) The next year, the brewery was out of business.

It wasn't until 1877, when the Memphis Brewing Company was established, that the brewing industry took hold in Memphis. It was on June 2, 1877 that Memphis Brewing Company served its first beer. (1/4) Odds are it was a lager, a style of beer that was sweeping the United States at that time. The Memphis Daily Appeal of July 31, 1877 noted the brewery was in full operation with S. Luehrmann, P. Wahl and H. Leisse in charge of the business. Prospects were good for the success of the enterprise. Sales for the month of August 1877 were 1,842 kegs ($9,555 at retail)

One of Memphis' finer hotels in the late 1800s was Luehrmann's. Henry Luehrmann was one of the city's first brewers, first with his own small brewery and later as the main bottler for Schlitz in the area. This tray promoted his hotel.

7

which was more than the amount of beer brought into the city during the same month the previous year. (1/5) By April of the next year, the brewery's payroll had reached 40 employees at an average wage of $2.25 a day. (1/6) For the first time in Memphis, a brewery was growing rapidly and making a profit. It was enough to attract a buyer. Or, in this case, three of them.

John Wolfgang Schorr was born in Bavaria and immigrated with his family to America when he was about 11 years old. Growing up in a family that had been in the brewing business for hundreds of years, John Schorr's career path was laid out for him. At an early age it was expected that someday he would make beer - lager beer in the Bavarian German style. His first brewing position would be under his father, Johan Schorr, in the small family brewery in Waterloo, Iowa. After he mastered the intricacies of the brewing business, he went to St. Louis, where he was employed by the Anthony & Kuhn Brewery. In 1872 he was made foreman of the brewery where he remained until 1878. He married Mary Haas whose beer brewing family was from St. Louis. John Schorr eventually bought an interest in the Excelsior Brewing Company in St. Louis (located at the current site of Union Station) and became vice president of the enterprise.

Beautiful four color lithography work is still as beautiful today as it was in 1900 when this picture was issued. The image is not original, the same picture exists in advertising for several other breweries. The printer would print hundreds of the pictures and then go back and add the name of the brewery that placed the order with them. This kept the printers costs down and the pieces were not sold to other breweries in the same area as the companies that had bought the lithos.

John Schorr's wife died in 1883, leaving him alone with their six small children. She was buried in the Schorr family plot in St. Matthew's Cemetery in St. Louis. He too was buried there, next to his first wife, after he passed away in 1932. However, he had a lot of living to do before then. Just shy of a year after Mary Schorr's death, on his 33rd birthday, John Schorr remarried. His intended bride, Gretchen Rachel Uhrig, was less than 18 years old when he proposed. Because she was under-age, he had to ask permission for her hand in marriage. Her mother Anna Uhrig agreed. The newlyweds didn't stay in St. Louis long, there was a brewery in Memphis that needed them.

Along with fellow St. Louis Germans Caspar Koehler (former co-owner of the Excelsior Brewery Company) and Peter Saussenthaler, John Schorr was looking to put his knowledge of the beer industry to work away from the crowded beer market of St. Louis. The three men learned of the success of the Memphis Brewing Company and went down for a look. It didn't take long for them to decide to make the visit permanent.

In 1885, Joseph Hadden was the mayor of Memphis and the popula-tion of the city was now near 62,000. Recent immigrants from several European countries had helped Memphis grow and recover quickly from the trials of the 1860s and 1870s. The city was

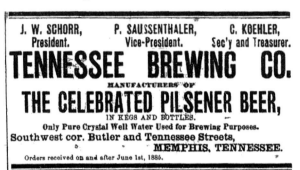

The new Tennessee Brewing Company ran this ad to let the public know that they were open for business. The ad appeared in *The Daily Memphis Avalanche*, May 29, 1885.

booming and had an expanding potential for business opportunities. As a small, profitable operation that could be purchased without a lot of money, the Memphis Brewing Company had enticing possibilities for the three Saint Louis men. It was exactly what they desired. On January 22, 1885, the Memphis Brewing Company was sold to Caspar Koehler, Peter Saussenthaler and John Schorr for $18,000. (1/7) Included in that amount was the brewery property at the corner of Tennessee Street and West Butler Avenue in the South Bluff section of the city. George H. Herbers, president of the Memphis Brewing Company, signed the papers on behalf of the sell-ers. Soon afterward, a new corporation was set up, the Tennessee Brewing Company, which would take over the brewery. On March 22, 1885, exactly two months after they bought the Memphis Brewing Company, the name of

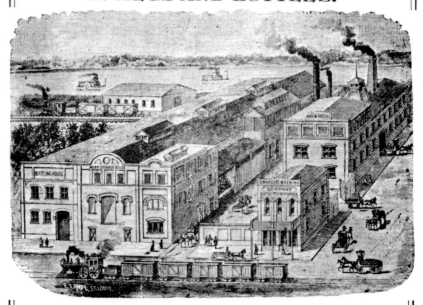
This full page ad in Dow's Memphis Directory for 1888 promoted the new company and its beer. The drawing of the brewery buildings is one that creates the impression that the brewery was larger than it really was. It is also interesting to note that the ad only promoted one type of beer. In the 1880s, few breweries bothered to give their beers names relying instead on types of beer.

10

the company changed. The papers to sell the Memphis Brewing Company to the Tennessee Brewing Company, a Tennessee corporation, for $28,000 (1/8) were signed by Caspar Koehler and his wife Josephine, Peter Saussenthaler and his wife Emilee and John W. Schorr and his wife Rachel. While there is no confirmed explanation for the difference in price, it is assumed that the additional money was used as operating capital. John Schorr would be the new corporation president, Peter Saussenthaler would be vice president and Caspar Koehler would be treasurer. Each man received approximately 33,000 shares of stock in the new company. (1/9) The secretary would be Adam Joseph Uhrig, John Schorr's brother-in-law.

The new owners had big plans for the little brewery. They immediately spent more than $40,000 for improvements to the brewery buildings and for new equipment, (1/10) increasing capacity to about 240 barrels a day. (1/11) The new company opened for business May 30, 1885. A formal opening was held that same day with a "street parade, musicians and a reception at the brewery where hundreds of invited guests were received by President Schorr." (1/12) More than 40,000 glasses of beer were served to the public that day. (1/13) Orders were being accepted for the company's Pilsener brand beer in bottles or kegs, (1/14) and approximately 15 people were on the payroll.

Despite the fanfare of the opening, the brewery and its location did not have the one key element needed for the new brewery to be a complete success, a constant source of quality water.

Drinking water of 1885 Memphis was way below the standards of today. Most drinking water still came from local creeks and rivers and shallow wells. Rain water was the best source of clear drinking water, but the heavens above would hardly supply a brewery with enough

The 1890s brought this stemmed pilsner glass from the Tennessee Brewing Company. This embossed glass was given out to saloon and tavern owners to use in their establishments. The glass turns a slight shade of purple if it gets too much sun as it ages.

water on a regular basis to be successful. A deep well was dug on the property in 1887. It was one of the first artesian wells in the city. The well tapped into water at 187 feet - a pure stream of crystal clear water which was at an ideal temperature for beer making. (1/15) The quantity of water was such that this same well was still being used by the brewery when it closed in 1954. Now there was little standing in the way of success for the new Tennessee Brewing Company.

Early on, space became a problem for the fledgling brewery. There simply wasn't enough of it. So between 1886 and 1890, an expansion program added a storehouse for the aging tanks and full beer kegs. In 1890, the remaining southern and middle sections were constructed. The three sections combined make up the building that still stands today. Each new addition was labeled with the name of its function and early photographs and drawings show the building names prominently displayed. New stables were also built

The brewery founders were proud of their German heritage and showed it in their use of the German Iron Cross on many of their early labels. This Special Brew Pilsener label was used around 1900. Note too the use of the phrase "Southern Enterprise." There was a big push to buy items made in the south in the late 1880s as the area further recovered from the economic disaster of the War Between the States.

across Tennessee Street. The brewery which had once been only on the corner now occupied half the block. The office for the brewery carried the address of 11 W. Butler Ave. but the new buildings had a different address, 477 Tennessee St. The new buildings were built in a Romanesque Revival style with limestone blocks forming the base of the front of the buildings and red brick walls, some 30 inches thick, above it. These buildings were meant to last.

Many years later the brewery grounds were still impressive. "I just loved the brewery," said Mary Lou Gaerig whose father, Wilfred Ryan, was an engineer at the brewery. "It was just awesome to go there. The cobblestones

The apparent principals of the brewery posed for this picture in the late 1890s. From left, Adam Joseph Uhrig, secretary; Caspar Koehler, treasurer; Peter Saussenthaler, vice president; and John W. Schorr, president. Collectors of breweriana lust over the great items also shown in this picture: corner signs, etched glasses, at least three different labels, lettered boxes and barrels, what appears to be a calendar in the lower part of the picture and a factory scene lithograph partially seen hanging above the door.

Photo from Memphis: A Pictorial History by Kitty Plunkett, 1976. Used with permission of The Donning Company/Publishers of Virginia Beach, Va.

as you entered. The courtyard. The architecture. To a child, that building was really something." (1/16)

And, it was a good thing the expansion was underway. On August 11, 1888, there was a fire in one of the original buildings. It seemed to start on the roof of the bottling department and a storeroom to the rear and south side of the brewery. The origin of the fire was unknown, but the theory was that a spark from a railroad locomotive which passed by the brewery on a regular basis was the cause. A hops storage area and two beer cellars seemed to take the brunt of the fire. Fortunately, the hops and kegs of beer stored in those areas were removed before the fire reached them and destroyed that part of the building. A newspaper ad that appeared in the days following the fire suggested that it had not interrupted the brewery's business. John Schorr and his family were not so lucky. They lived in a house next to the brewery that was totally destroyed by the fire. Sparks driven by a southerly wind resulted in a fire that caused the total loss of the handsome, two

One of the first brands put out by the brewery, Pilsener helped establish the fledgling company in the marketplace. This label dates from around 1906.

This sales card dates from 1891-1892 and shows the Budweiser label (middle) that the Tennessee Brewing Co. made during those years. The other two labels are Export Lager (left) and Pilsener (right) which both show off the brewery founder's German heritage with the Iron Cross design.

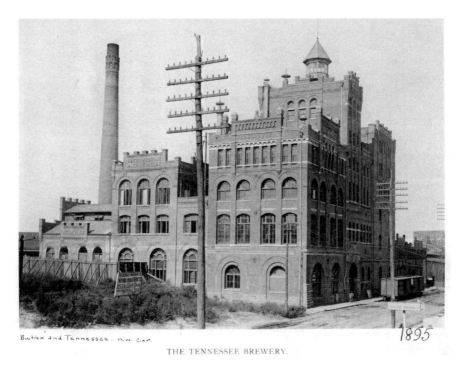

Butler and Tennessee. n.w. cor.   1895

THE TENNESSEE BREWERY.

This 1895 photograph shows the 1890 addition to the original Memphis Brewing Co. buildings. Note the name on the top of each part of the brewery noting what was done in each section and the railcar that was parked at the front of the brewhouse. *Photo courtesy of the Memphis/Shelby County Public Library and Information Center.*

story house. The insurance settlement from the fire was $15,000 for the brewery buildings and $5,600 for the house and its contents. (1/17) John Schorr and his family would go on to buy their own 90' x 264' lot on West Butler Avenue near the brewery (1/18) and build a home befitting the president of such a successful enterprise.

By 1892, business had increased dramatically. That year the Tennessee Brewing Company sold 36,132 barrels of beer. (1/19) The brewery had three brands of beer by then, Pilsener, Erlanger and Lager.   Another brand, Budweiser, made an appearance the year before. (1/20) It didn't survive long. Around this time, the Anheuser Busch Brewing Association of St. Louis was beginning to aggressively protect the tradename of its flagship brand which might have influenced Budweiser's short life as a Memphis beer. The wires of Memphis' fledgling telephone exchange reached the South Bluff area this year and the brewery had its first telephone with the number 649.

John W. Schorr's love of horses went past just owning thoroughbreds. He enjoyed riding them, too. He is shown here in this photo taken in Hot Springs, Ark. on a 1898 vacation with his wife Rachel (left) and youngest child Gertrude Anne (right).

The year also saw the brewery equipped to age 40,000 barrels in the cold storage house before delivery was made by one of 20 teams of horses kept in the stables. More than 100 men were employed with an annual payroll of $120,000. The brewery even had its own line of refrigerated rail cars that loaded on its track for points all over the south. Things were really looking up for the company. (1/21) The year 1892 also saw the beginning of the hobby for which John Schorr would become well-known - raising and running racehorses. It was in that year that he opened his stable of thoroughbreds with two. (1/22) The horses would be the first two of dozens over the ensuing years.

By 1897, John Schorr's stable required 24 stalls at Memphis' Montgomery Park (located in what is now the Mid-South Fairgrounds.) His stable had more racehorses than any other stable in the United States. (1/23) His horse, Lieber Karl, won the 14th running of the Tennessee Derby, a 1 1/8 mile race for 3-year-olds, in April of 1898. At that time, the Tennessee Derby was larger than the Kentucky Derby, attracting many of the same horses with a larger purse. Lieber Karl would finish second in the Kentucky Derby that year behind Plaudit, the best finish any of John Schorr's horses

16

SOUTHERN ❖ ENTERPRISE.

THE TENNESSEE BREWING CO.

IS THE LARGEST ESTABLISHMENT
OF ITS KIND IN THE SOUTH, ITS
CAPACITY BEING 250,000 BBLS.
EQUIPPED WITH THE LATEST
IMPROVEMENTS AND AS MODERN
AS ANY IN THE UNITED STATES.

BRANDS.

PILSENER BEER.
EXPORT BEER.
BUDWEISER BEER.
TENNESSEE PALE BEER.
BAVARIAN BEER
IN KEGS AND BOTTLES.
WARRANTED TO KEEP IN ANY
CLIMATE.

TENNESSEE BREWING CO.

MEMPHIS, TENNESSEE.
48

Old advertisements can help date brands from the brewery. Note the brands listed in this 1890 ad. This ad is the only reference the author has seen to two brands made by the brewery, Tennessee Pale and Bavarian.

would have out of the seven that raced at Churchill Downs. (1/24)

Memphis was rapidly returning to its former status as one of the shipping centers of the country. In 1893, the charter for the City of Memphis was reinstated largely due to the efforts of Robert Church, a former slave and the South's first African-American millionaire. Church bought the first Memphis bond to help the city get on its financial feet. He lived in a fine home on Beale Street, a business and cultural center for Memphis' black community for decades. He was best known for establishing the first park and auditorium for the city's black residents.

Memphis was really coming into its own, but another fire at the brewery in April 1895, again in the bottling department, was a minor setback for the company. The fire caused a $10,000 loss for the brewery, (1/25) but didn't slow production down one bit. Export brand bottled beer was introduced and distributed as the brewery's first beer outside the State of Tennessee.

A few years later the brewery lost two of its original founders. The sec-

This 1900 ad proclaimed the brewery as the largest one in the south. *Photo courtesy of the Memphis/Shelby County Public Library and Information Center.*

retary of the brewery, Joseph Uhrig died in March of 1898. John Schorr's son, Jacob Baltaser Schorr, was promoted to succeed him. (1/26) The corporate vice president, Peter Saussenthaler, passed away in December of 1899, and Caspar Koehler would be appointed to fill his spot. Koehler's former position, that of treasurer, would be added to John Schorr's title. (1/27) By 1900, the brewery's maximum capacity was increased to handle 100,000 barrels per year under the tutelage of Brewmaster Louis Schumacher. Payroll included 1,500 men and there was a fleet of 20 wagons to deliver half-barrel kegs to local saloons. The brewery had its own electric generating plant and an ice plant capable of making 30 tons of ice a day.

Ads claimed the Tennessee Brewing Company operated the largest brewery in the South. (1/28) The distribution area for the company's two bottled beers, Columbian Extra Pale and Erlanger, had grown to include five states, Tennessee, Arkansas, Mississippi, Alabama and Georgia (1/29) with sales reaching 45,929 barrels. (1/30) Columbian had first been introduced in 1893 after it reportedly won first prize in a special competition at the World's Columbian Exposition in Chicago. By winning the prize, the special brew could be named Columbian, the only beer by that name ever sold.

18

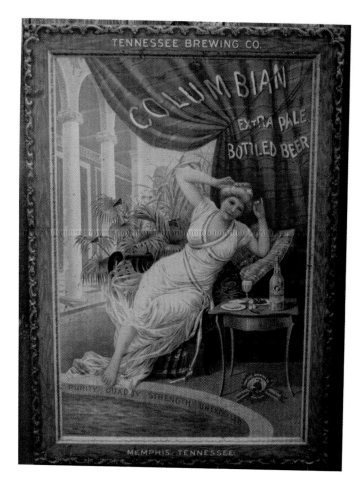

Self framed tin signs were very popular with breweries in the late 1800s. The Tennessee Brewing Company issued this one to promote its Columbian Extra Pale Beer which reportedly won the top prize at the World's Columbian Exposition in Chicago. By winning, this beer was the only American brand to carry the name.

By 1902, additional ice machines had been added bringing the daily output of the brewery up to 35 tons. The brewery had also built its own cooperage and drilled another artesian well. (1/31) John Schorr added new titles to his name while serving as second vice president and director of the Mercantile Bank of Memphis (1/32) and as vice president for the Germania Insurance Company of Memphis. (1/33)

John Schorr's prominence was assured in Memphis, and the Schorr family was notable in the community for its service, brewery and racehorses. The casual onlooker was also impressed by the Schorr horses and carriage that sauntered through the streets of Memphis each afternoon. A young boy named Walter Chandler, who grew up to be mayor of Memphis and a U.S. Congressman, reminisced in a December 20, 1956 article in the Memphis Commercial Appeal about what he remembered seeing as a child.

Probably the most commonly seen sign from a brewery from which nothing was very common, this pre prohibition tin sign is in lots of collections. This is mostly due to a box of them that was found in the 70s still wrapped in the paper they shipped in to the brewery. Signs from this box are notable because they all have a bad spot in the lower left hand corner from water damage.

"Shelby Street (now Front Street) was a place of flowers and trees and interesting people. Tall sycamores lined the moss covered brick sidewalks, and giant magnolias bloomed in the yards of stately mansions. Every afternoon, weather permitting, two spirited horses drawing a stylish Victoria were driven out of an immaculate residence on Butler Street (now Avenue) and turned east on Shelby. John W. Schorr, president of the brewery, famous horseman and philanthropist, and his wife were taking their customary ride, with, occasionally, one or two of their pretty daughters sitting opposite them. In the driver's seat was a liveried servant, black as midnight but proud as Lucifer – Osie, by name. Looking very much like the Kaiserin of Germany, Mrs. Schorr was always handsome in a picture hat and driving costume, with a parasol overhead while Mr. Schorr wore a gray bowler, a tight fitting cutaway suit and gloves to match. They made a distinguished looking couple, and with much dignity, drove briskly up the thoroughfare and out of sight. In an hour, precisely, they returned as they went, and the ride was over, but the memory of it lingered in the mind of a small boy who watched in wonder from a yard on the corner. Surrounded by Germans who lived near and worked for the brewery, the Schorr mansion might have been likened to a little

The label on this bottle is different from the one shown on the tin sign above promoting the brand. This one dates around 1906-1907 and was the last Columbian label used.

castle in the Vaterland, with the neighborhood a small principality in itself." (1/34)

John Schorr's racehorses were beginning to take his time away from the brewery. He and his wife traveled the country extensively, following their horses from track to track. From San Francisco to Miami, from Saratoga to Seattle, the colors of the Schorr stable, an orange shirt with black sleeves and a white cap, were seen all over the country. By 1903, the brewery even had its own featured race at Montgomery Park, the Tennessee Brewing Company Stakes, a seven furlong contest for 3-year-olds and up. (1/35) On opening day at the new Oaklawn Park in Hot Springs,

This lithograph is the older of the two shown in this book judging from the lady's clothing. Notice that the brewery's name was placed on the edge of the litho. This made the picture more palatable to hang in one's parlor or saloon. Advertising pieces of its day were very subtle compared with those of today.

Ark. (Feb. 24, 1905) one of John Schorr's horses, Duelist, won the inaugural race in front of 3,000 people. (1/36) The brewery was doing well, affording the Schorr's the resources to maintain both their stable and travel. But the winds of change were right around the corner.

In 1906, the State of Tennessee outlawed gambling on horses. With that new law came the demise of the Tennessee Derby, which had a larger purse than its now better known cousin the Kentucky Derby. With no place to race in Memphis, John Schorr allowed the size of his stable to decrease.

John Schorr's love of racehorses, however, never diminished, and the September 1909 issue of The American Brewer noted that Schorr was "again to enter the racing game on a large scale."

With his son John Farley Schorr as his trainer and jockey Tommy Burns, one of the most successful jockeys in America, under contract, John Schorr was determined to make his mark. That he did. By 1912, he was crowned

Serving trays were very popular ways to advertise breweries. They were attractive and caught the customer's eye, plus they were functional as a way to carry more bottles of beer to customers. This oval tray (top) is the only one known to exist today although it probably has at least a twin judging from the paint specs found on the back of the tray. A difficult find for collectors, about a dozen of the rectangle tray (below) have survived since it came out around 1903. Both trays show the actual brewery buildings, slightly embellished as was the norm of that time.

America's Champion Owner, winning more money than any other stable in the country. Then, he did it again in 1914 by winning more than $85,000. In 1915, John Schorr's horse Goldcrest Boy finished 12th out of 16 horses in the Kentucky Derby. Schorr had two horses in that year's Derby, the other being named after his politician friend Ed Crump. It would be his last attempt at winning the largest prize among horse races. By 1916, John Schorr had sold all his horses and broken up his stable. In 1930, he burned his meticulous records and noted that he had won enough in purses to slightly more than pay the operating expenses for his stable over the years. (1/37)

John W. Schorr at his desk. Note the race horse picture and items on his desk. Even at work, horseracing was still one of his passions. This picture probably dates from the 1890s.

The winds of change for the brewery began to blow when a competitor, the first to directly challenge the Tennessee Brewing Company, showed on the horizon. Several other Memphians saw the success that Tennessee Brewing was having and wanted to start their own brewery. The Memphis Brewing and Malting Company was formed and built a new $300,000 plant on the corner of Winchester and Concord in Memphis. (1/38) Opening January 28, 1907, the new concern boasted of its own power plant and ice plant. Brewmaster W. Schiefferdecker put out a new brew called Pearl of Memphis in bottles and kegs. (1/39) The brewery even had its own inaugural march titled "The Pearl of Memphis" written by Gabriel Katzenberger especially for its opening. Luckily no amount of pomp and circumstance could take business away from the Tennessee Brewing Company. Within 10 months of its grand opening, the creditors of the Memphis Brewing and

A real one of a kind piece, this tray (top) is one of the few advertising items that the Memphis Brewing and Malting Co. produced. This label (below) is the only label known that was used by the Memphis Brewing and Malting Co. The Pearl of Memphis brand and the brewery that made it both lasted 3 1/2 years, from 1907-1910.

Malting Company asked for and received involuntary bankruptcy for the firm. (1/40) It struggled on until September of 1910 (1/41), even changing its name in June of 1909 to the Memphis Brewing Company. (1/42) In the end, the reputation and business that John Schorr and his company had built was just too much to overcome.

A fire on August 19, 1906 would again set the Tennessee Brewing Company back briefly. The entire bottling department went up in smoke, a $30,000 loss. (1/43) When rebuilt, the department would have three bottling

John W. Schorr's passion for horses was also evident in this 1890's label. The brand is interesting because of the horse racing connection. The label is interesting because it is the only oval label produced by the brewery.

lines capable of 1,250 pints per hour (1/44) and one machine with the latest technology available- a crown capper. Now customers could open their bottles of beers more easily, without the need of a corkscrew. New brands were introduced, Faultless and Goldcrest. The latter of the two became the brewery's flagship trade name and lasted until the company folded in 1954. A new brew master, Valentine "Vollie" Schorr, the nephew of John Schorr, joined the firm in 1908. Business was booming with 80,149 barrels sold that year. (1/45) One could buy a keg of beer for $11 plus tax. Several buildings located close to the brewery were destroyed May 20, 1908, by fire, but this time the brewery went largely undamaged, despite the serious scare.

"The half million dollar brewery was threatened for more than an hour after the flames spread to the Orgill Brothers Warehouse (next door to brewery across Schorr's Alley)," said the Commercial Appeal newspaper the

Felt pennants were an inexpensive advertising item for breweries although few used them. The Tennessee Brewing Co. made two, both pre-prohibition. The one on the left features a bottle of Goldcrest Beer whose label helps date it to around 1906-1907. The second felt pennant highlights the brewery's logo of the man sitting on a cotton bale. Nothing is know about the origin of this logo.

Notice this pennant hanging up on the mirror of the saloon postcard shown below. It probably pre-dates the other pennant by a couple of years. Both pennants shown are the only examples of them known to have survived. The exact location of the saloon is unknown.

The exact date that this brand was bottled is unclear but it appears that Faultless Beer came out between 1907 and 1909. The label has the Food and Drug Act of 1906 line on it. This one is the only known Faultless label and makes it a super addition to a collection despite the torn part missing from its top.

Another example of a pre-Prohibition label from the brewery, reportedly the first for what would become itís flagship brand, Goldcrest.

This small envelope contains a four-color logo for the brewery. No envelope produced for the brewery after this one used more than two colors.

next day. "(The brewery) only sustained very slight damage from flying sparks and excessive heat." John Schorr, watching the fire from his home a half block away, "finally collapsed suffering almost a complete breakdown." (1/46) The brewery's 30 inch thick walls between it and the warehouse next door saved it.

In the summer of 1909, a new brand of Tennessee Brewing Company beer was introduced, Schorr's Fermented Beverage. It was a non-intoxicating brew aimed to appease the groups of the day railing against alcohol. (1/47) What fires and a direct competitor could not do, an organized group of tee-totalers did. Eventually. Driven by the Women's Temperance Union, prohibition forces were gaining strength in the country. By 1910, the Tennessee General Assembly had passed a bill, over Gov. Malcolm Patterson's veto, to forbid the manufacture of intoxicating beverages and the sale of liquor within four miles of any school in the state. July 1910 also saw company vice president Caspar Koehler die while on a trip to Berlin, Germany. His son Julius H. Koehler took his place as corporate vice president.

In 1912, the ownership of the company was transferred from the Tennessee Brewing Company, a Tennessee corporation, to the Tennessee Brewing Company, a business trust. This move was made to protect the personal assets of the owners and included all the buildings and inventories on hand. Officials in the state's four largest cities, Memphis, Nashville, Knoxville and Chattanooga made little effort to enforce the new law. Bars in Memphis operated openly. In 1912, the City of Memphis even licensed liquor dealers. In 1915, the State Senate impeached the Shelby County (Memphis) attorney general and a Shelby County judge for refusing to uphold the prohibition laws. Memphis Mayor Edward H. Crump was even removed from office by the courts in 1916 for his refusal to enforce the prohibition laws. The enforcement of prohibition was inevitable in Memphis. Tennessee Gov. Thomas C. Rye pushed through legislation in 1917 called the "bone-dry" bill. It made it illegal to transport liquor into or out of the state. Then in 1919,

Used both in the brewery's boardroom and in saloons all over its trade area, this super acid etched glass is a tough find today.

Tennessee's General Assembly ratified the national Prohibition amendment with only four dissenting votes. (1/48)

By the time national prohibition hit, the Tennessee Brewing Company had undergone numerous changes in an attempt to stay afloat, but these changes could not keep the company alive for long.

This 12 ounce clear glass embossed bottle dates before prohibition and before the addition of the crown capper machine at the brewery in 1906. This bottle would have been sealed with a cork stopper.

This self-framed tin sign is from the period between 1906 and 1912. Advertising featuring pretty girls and mythical characters was a popular way to promote a brewery's product.

Chapter Two

For a brewery, state and national prohibition was a deathblow. Cut out of manufacturing its only product, the Tennessee Brewing Company eventually would fold. But not before it was forced to.

The brewery made its last batch of Goldcrest Beer in 1913. A letter to the stockholders of the company notes the last beer was brewed October 15, 1913. However, a letter from John Schorr to Leo Rassieur, one of the company's directors, stated that they "did not manufacture anything after the first quarter of 1914 excepting trial brews of eighty two hundred barrels of a temperance drink called Brewette but did manufacture in 1913 approximately its normal production of beer." Whichever date is correct, the 527 men on the payroll at the time were laid off, (2/1) but some of them wouldn't be unemployed long.

The company letterhead during prohibition looked a lot like that which was used before the "great experiment" took effect. Note the brand names for cereal beverages, ginger ale and pure barley malt syrup, the basic ingredient of home-brewed beer.

It has been said that whoever named the low alcohol product "near beer" had a poor sense of distance. But it was the closest thing that the Tennessee Brewing Company could make to its popular beers. Survival was the focus of the brewery's management. After just six weeks of being closed, the brewery reopened making "near beer." This effort would only last a short time. The 1915 City Directory for Memphis shows John Schorr as president and treasurer, Julius H. Koehler as vice president, Jacob Schorr as

Sales of NIB weren't limited to the Memphis area. This ad appeared in an El Paso, Tex. newspaper in 1920.

secretary and Val Schorr as brewmaster. This management team would outlive the brewery. A letter written July 19, 1915 to the Internal Revenue Service said "we will close down our plant in about a week or ten days and will have on hand a little over 1,000 barrels of "near beer" which is no good and will have to be dumped into the sewer."

A follow-up letter to the Internal Revenue Service on August 3, 1915 stated that the company had gone out of business. The huge buildings wouldn't sit quiet for long. A new concern, the Goldcrest Company, which would manufacture soft drinks, was started in late 1915 in the old brewery buildings. Fred Uhrig, John Schorr's brother-in-law was the new company president and Irving E. Calhoun was secretary. (2/2) After less than two years, they gave up the business, and the buildings again sat idle.

It was hard for the men of the brewery to sit still. Regardless of the laws, they needed to work. A second attempt was made to make something of the company and its plant. On February 16, 1917, John Schorr, Jacob Schorr, Fred Uhrig, I.E. Calhoun and A.J. Calhoun applied for a charter for a new concern, the Tennessee Beverage Company. (2/3) The charter would be approved and the new business was incorporated the following month. April 15, 1917 was the first day the new company was open for business. (2/4) It made two cereal beverages, NIB, which stood for non-intoxicating beverage, and Goldcrest, and soft drinks including root beer. NIB was the company's best seller. By the first quarter of 1918, 13,340 barrels of NIB were manufactured. Sales territories included the areas formerly served with beer and new ones, such as the State of Oklahoma opened in 1918 (2/5) and El Paso, Texas in 1920. (2/6)

When the author found this bottle in a Hot Springs, Ark. flea market it answered the question of what bottles did the company use during Prohibition. This embossed bottle looks very similar to soft drink bottles and was probably used for products other than near beer which would have been sold in bottles that resembled beer.

The chrome wire opener was used to promote NIB.

Sales never reached the numbers generated by beer sales. By 1926, total sales shrunk to just $167,977 which produced a loss for the company of more than $10,000. (2/7) Just 17 hourly employees remained on the job. (2/8) The attempt to keep business going reached a point of no return in 1927. Only Jacob Schorr and Fred Uhrig wanted to continue in business. By 1928, the company would lose more than $46,500. It was time to give up. The company itself stayed in business, but only on paper. The remaining contract to manufacture soft drinks, with Canadian Dry Ginger Ale, was canceled effective December 31, 1928. (2/9) All of the remaining employees were laid off and the plant mothballed. John Schorr's main interest at this point

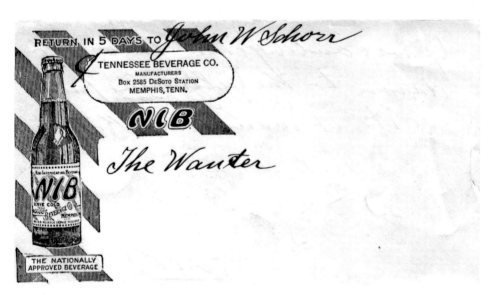

Very few items remain from the Prohibition version of the brewery. This envelope is unique in two ways. First, it's the only envelope known to have survived from the Tennessee Beverage Co. and second, it contains the signature of John W. Schorr.

was salvaging something out of the mess Prohibition had made of his company. "We have a capacity in the Brewhouse of 350 barrels a day with cold storage capacity of 24,000 barrels," he wrote the Meyer Supply Company of St. Louis on Dec. 4, 1929. "The whole plant is for sale at a very low price."

In 1930, John Schorr and his wife Rachel moved out of their fine home next to the empty brewery buildings to live at the William Len Hotel in Memphis. There he would die at the age of 80 on May 20, 1932 after suffering a heart attack four weeks earlier. (2/10) He left all of his seemingly worthless stock in the Tennessee Brewing Company to his wife and none to any of his children. (2/11) Family lore has had it for years that John Schorr tore down his home on Butler Avenue when he moved from it because he did not want anyone else living in it. (2/12) Facts prove otherwise, as the home was being rented out as late as 1947 for the princely sum of $30 a month.

John Schorr had seen the rise of his brewery to one of the largest in the country. He had seen his horses win dozens of races through the years. He had seen his adopted hometown grow to more than a quarter million people. But he would not live long enough to see Prohibition end, and his brewery reopen. That would be the legacy of his son, Jacob Schorr.

NIB, short for non intoxicating beverage, was the primary brand of the Prohibition version of the brewery. Aside from selected southern states, NIB was also sold in Oklahoma as evidenced by this tin sign (above) that was found in an Oklahoma City antique mall in the late 1980s. The colors of gold and green stripes with black lettering is a combination that only a collector could love.

This small tin over cardboard sign (below) was used to promote NIB. Another version of this sign exists today that replaces the company logo in the upper left-hand corner with a picture of a paddle wheeler.

acob Schorr knew that the beer business could be very good to a fellow. Prior to Prohibition, the Tennessee Brewing Company had been very successful. Now, Franklin Roosevelt, the new president of the country, made a pledge to end the "Great Experiment." It didn't take long for Congress to repeal the Volstead Act, which created Prohibition. The country went "wet" again with the ratification of the Twenty First Amendment on December 5, 1933. The only question about John Schorr's legacy was how to get the vacant brewery on the corner of Tennessee Street and West Butler Avenue back in business. More importantly, a way had to be found to finance the project.

Each of the stockholders in the company put up for sale an equal amount of stock to raise cash. (3/1) Additional funding came from several private individuals who saw an opportunity to invest in a winner. Jacob

John W. Schorr's home on W. Butler Ave. was one of the finest in Memphis at the outset of the 20th century. The office of the brewery sat right next door. Note the brewery buildings looming in the background.

Goldcrest Beer
Tennessee Brewing Co.
MEMPHIS

What appears to be a plastic tongue depressor is actually a piece with a history. In saloons of the early 1930s, patrons usually ordered a beer that was a draught poured into a glass. This foam scraper was used to scrape the excess foam off the top. By the mid 1930s, the health department folks decided that this was an unsanitary practice and foam scrapers disappeared. This one is made of bakelite, an early form of plastic, and probably dates from 1933 or 1934.

Schorr approached several friends of his family, the largest investor of which was one Charles Zilker of San Antonio, Texas who would invest in other breweries in later years such as the Spearman Brewing Company in Pensacola, Florida. Within days, the money was in hand to refurbish the vacant Memphis brewery and get it back to making beer, but there was a small matter to clear up first. Someone else had applied for a charter under the name of Tennessee Brewing Company.

Wanting to protect the old corporate name, Jacob Schorr immediately filed a lawsuit. Two Memphians, Lowell Taylor and W.C. Lanning claimed the name Tennessee Brewing Company was available since the company had changed its name to the Tennessee Beverage Company. Jacob Schorr and his partners disagreed. Fortunately for them, the court ruled in their favor and the old corporate name stayed with its original owners. (3/2) Armed with $200,000 in capital, Lowell Taylor and W.C. Lanning filed for a charter using a different name – the Memphis Brewing Company. (3/3) They disappeared soon afterward, never to produce a single barrel.

By June of 1933, work at the Tennessee Brewing Company was going full speed. A new company charter was prepared and about 100 men were working around the clock on the renovations. More than $75,000 was spent getting the brewery back in working order, (3/4) and by August, it was ready. The owners were prepared to see their first batch of beer brewed in nearly 20 years come off the line. It would be named Goldcrest.

November 9th was a day that a lot of people had looked forward to, but none any more than Ernest Kuehn, Sr. "When the brewery closed, my grandfather went to work as a policeman," said Eleanor Kuehn Scott. "When the brewery reopened, he quit being a policeman and went right back to work selling beer. There was never any doubt that he'd go back to the brewery."

Eleanor Scott's family was well connected to the brewery. In addition to her grandfather, her great uncle Julius Kuehn worked in the bottling plant for more than 50 years and her dad, Ernest Kuehn, Jr. was an engineer for the brewery.

In an attempt to rekindle some of the sales and name awareness that Goldcrest Beer had developed before Prohibition, Old Original Goldcrest was introduced. Its formula had several different variations producing different alcohol levels which were necessary to work with the various state's laws of the early 1930s.

The reopening of the brewery was a major accomplishment that meant Tennessee Brewing Company libations would again be available. "Memphians slaked their thirst yesterday for the first time in (over) 15 years with beer brewed and bottled in Memphis, as the first bottled Goldcrest beer was delivered to retailers by the Tennessee Brewing Company," said the Commercial Appeal of November 10, 1933.

It had been a long, hard road getting the brewery back in operating condition. But one hurdle had yet to be cleared. Because of Tennessee law, the brewery could not make any beer stronger than 3.2 per cent (alcohol by weight). This put it at a disadvantage going head to head with other brands

Goldcrest Super Six Beer was named to compete with other breweries' product being sold in Tennessee whose manufacture was not regulated by the states archaic laws. The name "Super Six" implied that the beer was a higher alcohol percentage than the state law allowed to be made in Tennessee.

in states like Mississippi which allowed four percent beer. Intense lobbying was taking place in the Tennessee General Assembly but it would take until April 24, 1935 before the state would allow a return to the pre-Prohibition strength of five percent. Until then, the brewery salesmen just had to work harder to sell beer.

"I remember as a young girl, my granddaddy bringing home wads of cash with him from work after making his sales calls for the day," said Eleanor Kuehn Scott. "He would be out late a lot of nights and the brewery office had closed by the time he made his last call. So he'd just take the money in the next morning. My grandfather spoke German and Italian as well as English. He got along so well with most of the grocers and hotels and the like. A lot of them were immigrants and

Another of the brands that the brewery introduced in 1935, Goldcrest Special Beer, tried to capitalize on the Goldcrest brand name.

40

October 1935 brought the only product that carried the Schorr family name. Schorr's beer didn't last very long, disappearing in less than two years.

This was the first attempt by the brewery to make an ale, introduced in 1935. Notice the similar design for several of the labels of that year, Super Six, Goldcrest Lager and Pale Ale.

liked him because he could speak to them in their language. I suppose it helped him sell a lot of beer, too." (3/5)

Nationally, beer consumption was only half of what it had been in 1919, the year before Prohibition. (3/6) The Tennessee Brewing Company was bucking the national trend. It immediately started by coming out with new brands. In addition to Old Original Goldcrest, the brewery also created Goldcrest Super Six Beer in November of 1934. (3/7)

"Tennessee law prevented us from making or selling beer that was six per cent alcohol by weight," said E.C. "Buddy" Krausnick, Jr. who would become brewery president in 1953. "The law was changed to allow sales of six per cent beer in the state but it would have taken us at least 90 days to get it made, aged and ready for sale. The out of state breweries all had six per cent beer ready and waiting at the (state) border. Super Six Beer was a quick fix, meant to convince the public that the bottle contained more than it really did. It was the same beer as our other labels." (3/8)

As the company searched for the right brand to help it make a profit in the tough post-Prohibition marketplace, several new brands were introduced including Goldcrest Lager in early 1935.

Special Goldcrest Beer was introduced in February 1935 (3/9), Goldcrest Lager Beer in March 1935 (3/10) and Goldcrest Extra Pale Lager in November of 1935. (3/11) Goldcrest Pale Ale hit the shelves in April of 1935, the first ale ever made by the brewery. (3/12) A totally new beer, one lighter and less "hoppy" than its other brands, was developed. (3/13) Schorr's Extra Pale Beer would appear in October 1935. (3/14)

Display cards for the new brand featured a glass of beer and a bottle with the new Schorr's label under the slogan "It Schorr is Good Beer." (3/15) The Progress Sign Company of Cincinnati would receive several orders during 1935 for 3' x 5' outdoor metal signs for Goldcrest Beer featuring the slogan "There is No Better Beer." (3/16) But, despite the aggressive sales and

The location of Bill's Place is unknown but it is a good example of painted window ads that the brewery used extensively from 1933. On a side note, is there any kind of spaghetti other than Italian?

marketing posture the brewery was taking, finances continued to be tight. A December 19, 1935 letter from A.E. Kammerer, the corporation's treasurer, to Jacob Schorr summed it up well. "I have realized all along that the financial condition of the company was very unsatisfactory and that we were again suffering from a lack of working capital," he wrote. But by 1936, that had begun to change.

Sales for the year 1936 reached 41,080 barrels and the company made its first profit since reopening after Prohibition. A large part of the year's growth came from sales of the newly renamed flagship beer, Goldcrest 51, amended in March of 1936 to mark the company's 51st year in business. The name came from a suggestion made by Mrs. E. C. "Collie" Krausnick, the wife of the company's corporate secretary. (3/17)

The brewery's two bottling lines now had a capacity of 27,000 bottles an hour. (3/18) A new 365 barrel copper brew kettle was installed, one of the country's largest (3/19) and additional delivery trucks were added to meet demand. (3/20) The new formula Goldcrest 51 recipe first introduced in late

This diecut cardboard sign was used in 1936 as it features the label with the phrase "Over 51 years of perfect brewing." Few of this sign have survived the years.

1938 was selling well. Its new lighter, milder, less "hoppy" taste was a hit. (3/21)

This was all very satisfying to Jacob Schorr. Before Prohibition, he had been in the shadow of his father. But this new company was his to lead. He could relish its success as only one can when it's been earned.

Jacob Schorr had paid his dues in the brewing industry. Though born into a family that traced its brewing roots back to his great, great grandfather's brewery in Bavaria, (3/22) he chose to get much of his initial experience in other breweries. Jacob Schorr graduated from Wahl-Henius Institute in Chicago, one of the country's leading brewing schools, in 1894. (His son, Jacob B., Jr. would follow in his father's steps and graduate from Wahl-Henius in 1936.) For the next three years, Jacob Schorr went to Europe

This is the only tin over cardboard sign that has been found from the Tennessee Brewing Co. Its size is 11 1/2"w x 5 1/2"h. The condition isn't the best but it was found nailed up to an old country grocery store in southern Arkansas in the late 1980s. The style of lettering used and the price per bottle of 10 cents would date this sign from the late 1930s.

where he both worked and studied. He graduated from the Munchener Brauerakademie (Munich Beer Academy) in Munich, Germany and worked at various European breweries including the Union Brewing Company, Dortmund, Germany; the Actin Brewery, Pilsen, Bohemia; the Weissbear Brewery, Berlin; the Veringigti Brewery, Frankfort-On-Main, Germany; the Munich Brewery, Munich and others. In 1897, he was employed at the Blatz Brewing Company, Milwaukee but he would only stay there a year. (3/23)

It was time to join the family brewery and prepare himself for his turn at the helm. Although he was never more than a minor stockholder in the company himself, he wanted to make his mark. One of his two sons, Jacob B. Schorr, Jr. would follow him to the brewery in the years to come. The other son, Harry Dane Schorr, was a gifted athlete who was All-Memphis in baseball and football and turned down a scholarship to the University of Tennessee to pursue his first love – drawing. He would later work for the Hal Roach Studios in Hollywood. (3/24)

Jacob Schorr was serious about his company and, although kind, meant business.

"I used to ride home from work with Mr. (Jacob) Schorr (Sr.)" reminisced Doris Brigance Dolan who handled accounts payable in the brewery office from 1944-54. "He lived three short blocks from me. He was a good man. He could really bite your head off one minute and the next minute he'd be nice to you. He was tough but we all liked him. (3/25)

"I remember my dad referring to Mr. Schorr as 'that hard-headed German'," said Jane Howell whose father Jim Scott painted signs for the brewery. "He did work for the brewery for years so they must have worked things out between them." (3/26)

Jacob Schorr Sr. made strong impressions on just about everyone with whom he came into contact, especially his grandson.

"One of the fondest memories I have as a child was my grandfather Schorr taking me down to Beale Street," reminisced Jacob B. "Jake" Schorr III. "He took me everywhere and introduced me to everyone. He knew almost everybody by their first names. Mr. Jake, he was called. He taught me a valuable lesson that is still with me to this day and that's to treat everyone the same regardless of who they are. He followed that rule his whole life." (3/27)

Near Forrest City, Ark., along the Highway between Memphis and Little Rock was Jim's Place. This postcard has a postmark of April 4, 1939 from a traveler that stayed at Jim's. Note the Goldcrest sign hanging out front to the right of a Falstaff neon.

Despite a strong desire to see the brewery succeed, there were some things the leadership of the company was not willing to attempt. During the late 1930s, a new type of packaging was making some real waves in the brewing industry. For years, can companies had toyed with the idea of a metal bottle or can for beer and other drinks. As early as 1909, the American Can Company was experimenting with just such a container for beer. It wasn't until 1933 that a workable can was developed and January of 1935 before it would be put on the market. (3/28) A metal beer can would solve one of the brewing industry's biggest hurdles- the breakable glass bottle. Metal cans would not break, would cool down quickly and could be taken to places where glass bottles were not appropriate. It also might eliminate some injuries suffered by company employees.

The actual date that this token was used or its purpose isn't clear but is estimated to be from the 1930s. It is speculated that this was used as a promotion piece that could be passed out to the public. Odds are it will never be known how this brass token the size of today's nickel was used.

The back side of the token.

"I remember one really hot day we were filling steinie bottles," recalled Richard Campbell who had a summer job at the brewery between high school and college in 1948. "The glass in those was real thin. The only job in the bottling department that was not automated was removing the finished bottles from the labeler and packing them in the cartons. You'd pull six at a time and pack them. This one hot day, I pulled six out and one of them exploded in my hand. I nearly fainted, it scared me so bad. Once I sat down and washed the blood off my hands, I realized that the only real damage was some glass shards that were sticking out. If that sort of thing happened today, there would be inquiries, workman's comp claims and everything else. Back then, I went back to work so I wouldn't lose out on the $1.47 an hour." (3/29)

Cans would also be another expense that the brewery would not wish to tackle just yet. The additional equipment would be more than the officers of the brewery felt possible to afford. It would be 1948 before beer cans would be used by the Tennessee Brewing Company. Until then, they would be a sales advantage that the competition would have at its disposal.

"We were late getting the equipment to can beer," said E. C. "Buddy" Krausnick, Jr. the company's last president. "If you didn't have it before the war started, you had to wait in line like we did."

But as the decade ended, the lack of Goldcrest Beer in cans was a minor problem compared to what was about to happen. While sales continued to grow to 53,864 barrels by 1939, the winds of war in Europe were about to sweep over the United States and dramatically affect the Tennessee Brewing Company.

E. Jungenfeld & Co. was a St. Louis architectural and engineering firm that specialized in designing breweries and other similar industrial plants in the late 1800s. They published a book in the 1890s showing many of the buildings they had designed including a page of the Tennessee Brewing Company's buildings.

Chapter Four

War was raging in Europe in the 1940s, but it didn't stop the brewery from experiencing continued growth. In July of that year, a new 26 ton Meyer Dumore bottling line, a machine that took up an entire rail car for shipment to the plant, was installed. New fermenting and storage vats were also installed as part of a brewery expansion and plant improvement program begun the year before. (4/1) Goldcrest 51 and Goldcrest Ale were selling well and the brewery was showing its stockholders a profit. But the war wouldn't leave America alone for long.

The mood of Americans toward the war in Europe was that it just wasn't their war to fight. An isolationist attitude permeated the fabric of the United States until December 7, 1941. The Japanese attack on Pearl Harbor changed that, and brought America into the war full-force.

The war years were difficult for brewers. Hops, much of which was grown in Europe, was harder to find. All the ingredients of Goldcrest Beer, rice, corn, malt and yeast, were rationed and support items, such as beer boxes, were hard to get. Trucks could not be replaced during this time

Wooden boxes were the common way to ship the longneck returnable bottles that most beer was sold in by the brewery. This one dates back to the pre-Prohibition era which is obvious by its health claim of "pure food health beer," something the law would not allow after Prohibition.

because manufacturing plants were converted to provide vehicles for the war effort. Breweries simply had to keep repairing the trucks they had. And to top it all off, a huge portion of the workforce was sent overseas.

The Tennessee Brewing Company didn't have it any better than other brewers. Aside from the shortages of materials, the shortage of manpower was of utmost concern. A total of 39 of the brewery's employees, a staggering 20 percent of the men on the payroll, served in the armed forces during WWII. Two would never return home. Without the experienced men to operate the plant, the brewery turned to women and unskilled labor, with mixed results. Prior to the war the only women employed by Tennessee Brewing Company worked in the office. The necessity of employing women and unskilled labor in the brew house meant the workforce was highly inexperienced. With these green laborers, problems on the line occurred more frequently.

Any chance of seeing Goldcrest 51 Beer in a can was shot for nearly 10 years, as all available metal went to the war effort. In fact, the brewery participated in several tin drives during the war years. It's actually surprising that any of the brewery's pre-1940 metal advertising signs

The Memphis Commercial Appeal ran a weekly contest during the college football season for its readers to pick the winners. The brewery supplied the prizes for the people who did the best job, giving them a choice between a case of Goldcrest 51 Beer and Goldcrest Ale.

During the war, metal for signs was had to come by so cardboard signs became more prevalent. This one came out in 1944 in a self-framed design.

survived the war. Paper advertising was used more as cardboard signs, such as a 1944 pretty girl and horse sign (above), became more common. (4/2) The brewery sponsored bowling and softball teams in Memphis for the first time and, (4/3) Russwood Park, home of the Memphis Chicks, would see a Goldcrest 51 ad on the left center field fence. (4/4)

The public was forced to deal with the rationing of all sort of food items and other daily necessities. Fortunately, beer was not one of those things that was rationed, but it could be hard to find sometimes. American brewers were required by the U.S. government to sell 15 percent of their product to the armed services. This made things tough for breweries since they were producing less beer due to the shortages of materials.

"It all had to be 3.2 percent beer (alcohol content)," said E.C. "Buddy" Krausnick, Jr. "I remember dad saying many times that it wasn't very profitable and the brewery was darn glad to be done selling it to them after the war."

The Mid-South was home to several military bases and support facilities such as the Memphis Depot. There were also six Prisoner of War Camps in neighboring Arkansas. These camps, filled with German prisoners, had to be supplied with beer. (4/5)

It is said that necessity is the mother of invention. That was never so true as during WWII. Simple items, like new bottle caps, could not be found. Manufacturers like Crown Cork & Seal took old crowns and refurbished them. As late as 1943, the Tennessee Brewing Company was looking for a harness so it could utilize horses and a wagon for local deliveries. (4/6) The brewery leadership petitioned the city, to no avail, to pave over the cobblestones right in front of the company on Tennessee Street to save wear and tear on the delivery trucks. In the spring of 1945, the labeling machine for bottles broke down and parts could not be obtained for weeks. The only solution was to sell beer with no labels on the bottles. Production of Goldcrest Ale ceased in 1945 and the

The brewery did its part to promote patriotism during World War II. This 1944 newspaper ad was hardly politically correct for today but it hit home in its day. The brewery ran a lot of similar ads during the war and promoted bond sales heavily.

green ale bottles used for that particular beer were sold to other brewers including Bloomer Brewing (Bloomer, Wis.), Brewery Corporation of America (Cleveland, Ohio) and the Miami Valley Brewing Company (Dayton, Ohio). (4/7) Business went on at the brewery, as best it could.

Sales of beer during the war years didn't grow much with all the hurdles of wartime measures. In 1945, sales had only increased by a little more than 3,000 barrels since 1942. Corporate profits had actually fallen during the war, from $97,649.25 in 1942 to $71,049.03 in 1945. (4/8) The best news about business during the war was that it hadn't shrunk and was still on solid footing. It was a good thing. Starting in late 1945, thousands of soldiers were returning and they had a strong desire for the creature comforts of home, including Goldcrest 51 Beer.

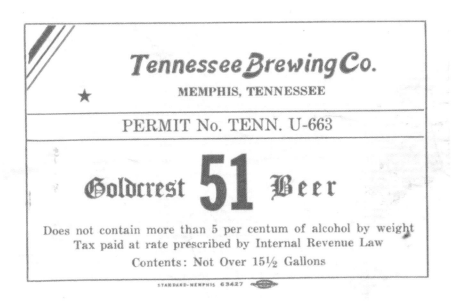

Primarily a draught beer seller before Prohibition, bottles and later cans took over from a cold glass at the local tavern. Kegs had to have labels, too, as evidenced by this one from the early 1940s.

*T*he war ended in 1945, but the shortages of materials and machinery persisted for years afterward. There were millions of people in Europe and Asia who needed to be fed and to see their war-torn countries rebuilt. Much of the food and materials to revitalize these war-weary citizens and their countries came from America.

The post-war years were exciting ones for the brewery despite the shortages it faced. Experienced workers were returning home. War-time shortages of the raw materials needed for making beer were finally easing. The demand for beer from returning servicemen and the deprived public meant that the brewery could sell as much beer as it could make. And then some.

Between August 1944 and October 1946, the Tennessee Brewing Company received dozens of inquiries from people wanting to set up distributorships and buy truckloads of beer. From San Francisco to Fredericksburg, Va., from Brooklyn to Miami, letters were received asking for beer. Unfortunately for the brewery, every one of the inquiries had to be declined. There simply wasn't enough beer to go beyond its usual trade area. Sharing with other parts of the country wasn't an option.

Chelsea Street in Memphis saw this billboard in the mid 1940's. Billboards were used by the brewery as early as around 1900. The last billboard ads for Goldcrest 51 Beer were up when the brewery announced its closing in 1954. *Photo courtesy of the Memphis/Shelby County Public Library and Information Center.*

The fact that the brewery was getting these letters from far off cities also meant that the local breweries in those areas were having the same challenges that Tennessee Brewing Company was experiencing.

Beer wasn't the only thing that was in short supply. An April 15, 1946 letter from George Meyer Manufacturing Company to the brewery owners notified them that "you have position number 40 out of a list of nearly 700

55

post war orders for bottling machinery." (5/1) During the war effort vehicles and their parts were tough items to get and those difficulties persisted after the war was over. The Tennessee Brewing Company eased its truck shortage by leasing vehicles from the Yellow Cab Company. Beginning in 1943, the brewery had leased trucks from them with a minimum of three (5/2) and a maximum of 15 (5/3) at a time. The delivery department would need every one of them in the years directly after the war.

In 1946, sales had reached 142,988 barrels and corporate profits were more than $190,000 for the year. A case of returnable 12 oz. bottled beer cost a retailer $1.87 plus 60 cents deposit. Every barrel made was sold as Goldcrest 51 Beer, as 51 Ale was discontinued in 1945. Neon signs, both indoor and outdoor were used for the first time, as were neon spectaculars, giant rooftop neons that were the size of highway billboards. (5/4) These were used in

This pint glass was made for the Schorr family and was used in their home. While it can not be fully substantiated, it is thought that the glass dates back to pre-Prohibition. The gold lettering is actually gold leaf.

Little Rock and Pine Bluff, Ark. and in Monroe, La., as well as in Memphis. One in particular, located at the corner of Union Avenue and Fourth Street in Memphis, stood out. It was 15 feet tall by 55 feet long. "It was the granddaddy of them all," said E.C. "Buddy" Krausnick, Jr. at this point a salesman for the brewery. "You could see it for miles."

Yet despite the many improvements made in the types of advertising pieces, much of the advertising was still hand-painted signs on the sides of the beer delivery trucks.

Other advertising used right after the war were "Presdwood" signs made by Grace Sign Company of Saint Louis, (5/5) both small and large sized plaster signs, (5/6) small metal die cut tacker signs, (5/7) several different cardboard signs, small plastic point of purchase signs (5/8) and 3' x 5' die cut metal signs (some beaded for better reflection). Wire openers were used for the first time (5/9) as were paper boxes for the returnable bottles. (5/10) Goldcrest 51 Beer became available in six-packs in September of 1946. (5/11) Billboards, newspaper ads and bus ads all used the slogan "Here's Your Number."

New distributors and areas were opened up for 51 Beer in Alabama, Arkansas, Louisiana, Mississippi and Tennessee. Brewery owned branches in Arkansas and Tennessee were expanded and new ones opened. New smokestacks were added to the brewery itself in September 1946 to handle the new boilers that had been installed, boilers that worked on gas instead of coal. Things were looking up for the brewery.

Outdoor neon signs were first used by the brewery soon after the end of World War II. This one was 3' wide by 5' high and was large enough to be seen a long distance away even during the day. At night, the red, gold and white lights of the sign could be seen even farther.

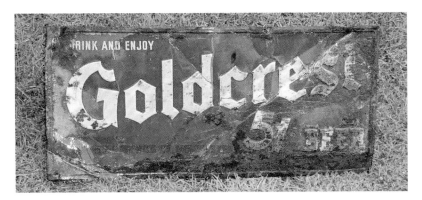

Once the raw material was available again after the war, the brewery used several metal signs to promote Goldcrest 51 Beer. This 13" high x 29" wide tin sign with embossed letters was found in a barn in northeast Arkansas in 2002.

When metal was in short supply, the brewery looked to other materials to make signs to promote Goldcrest Beer. Two sizes of plaster signs were made in 1946. This one is restored in the original colors of red, navy, gold and white.

Vince Coco worked with the Tennessee Brewing Company for many years. He worked both in the brewery's Arkansas branches and owned his own Goldcrest distributorship in Little Rock and El Dorado, Arkansas. He is shown here posing in front of a delivery truck in the mid to late 1940s. Note the headlight to his left. It is said that the state law in Arkansas did not require both headlights to work in that era and some enterprising marketing man, maybe Mr. Coco, saw an opportunity to promote his beer.

O n January 1, 1947, the Tennessee Brewing Company sat idle. The New Year's Day holiday had scattered the employees to their homes and families. They would toast each other with the hope of a good year to come. For the brewery, it would be the best year ever.

More than 200,000 barrels of beer were sold in 1947, (6/1) the most ever by the Tennessee Brewing Company. Goldcrest 51 Beer, or "51" as most people called it, was the dominant beer in Memphis and the mid-south area. Corporate profits that year, $528,123.24, (6/2) were the highest ever.

"I delivered a truckload of quarts to the Beale Street clubs two mornings a week," reminisced Ed Bretherick a route salesman with the brewery from 1945-54. "Then, I'd go back that afternoon with a truckload of pints. They sure bought a lot of 51 Beer from me." (6/3)

This aluminum diecut Goldcrest sign was first used in 1948.

The brewery's advertising agency, Merrill-Kremer, proposed the largest ad budget in the history of the brewery. Ads were seen in newspapers and on buses and taxis. They were heard

The brewery did not use many lighted signs to promote Goldcrest Beer but this panel is proof they did make some. This molded plastic panel could have been used in either a one or two sided sign designed in both indoor and outdoor versions.

on the radio and seen in movie theaters. New and exciting signs made their debut, including 9' outdoor neon signs, (6/4) 2' x 2' indoor "circle" neon signs, (6/5) plaster point of purchase signs, (6/6) menu boards, (6/7) small metal tacker signs, (6/8) larger rectangular metal signs (6/9) and both small and large sized plastic plaque point of purchase signs (6/10).

Not only did the brewery advertise with signs and radio ads, it also sponsored numerous sporting teams, from ladies bowling teams to softball, baseball and basketball teams in the Memphis area. (6/11) It was hard to go to a Cotton States League baseball game anywhere in the mid-south in the late 1940s and not see a Goldcrest 51 sign on the outfield fence. (6/12)

John Schorr's house at 15 W. Butler was still renting for $30 a month and the former cooper shop at 474 Tennessee St. was rented out as a restaurant for $25 a month. A customer could purchase 1/2 barrel of 51 beer for

Valentine "Vollie" Schorr (center, seated) was John W. Schorr's nephew and was brewmaster for the brewery until his retirement in 1948. At the far right in this picture is J.B. Schorr, Jr. the son of Jacob Schorr. J.B. Schorr would take over as brewmaster from his distant cousin Vollie. At the far left of the photo is Ernest Kuehn, Sr. The names of the men standing are unknown.

The corner of Madison and Cleveland in Memphis had a huge Goldcrest 51 neon sign in this picture taken January 2, 1948. The corner looks very different today and the sign is long gone. *Photo courtesy of the Memphis/Shelby County Public Library and Information Center.*

$10.50. (6/13) The brewery ordered ties and jackets for stockholders and staff. (6/14) Brewmaster Vollie Schorr retired and his nephew, J.B. Schorr, Jr. was promoted to his former position. (6/15) Vollie Schorr was well liked by others and would be missed.

"He was a true southern gentleman in every way," remembered Jack Borg, a cousin of Vollie Schorr. "Always immaculately dressed, always a real class act." (6/16)

New menu boards, (6/17) a point of purchase mirror, (6/18) new 8' x 10' and 10' x 12' outdoor metal signs, (6/19) die cut aluminum point of purchase signs, (6/20) "Tip For Good Taste" printed tip cards, (6/21) the last openers from the brewery, (6/22) and a new lighted Plexiglas sign, (6/23) the first for the brewery, all debuted in 1948.

Jacob B. Schorr headed up the brewery from 1933 until he retired in 1952. This photo dates around the time he retired. He would pass away in 1965 at the age of 88.

The year 1948 also saw Merrill-Kremer Advertising winning a first place award for designs it created for the brewery's billboards, (6/24) corporate president Jacob Schorr presented with an 'Honorary Life Membership' by the Master Brewers Association, (6/25) and the brewery establishing its own Federal Credit Union for employees. (6/26)

The brewery leadership started making plans for the future. Many of the brewery's original buildings dated from the 1880s and were in desperate need of being replaced. The new 12 and 32 oz. cans on the market were beginning to make inroads on the brewery's bottle and draught beer sales. The brewery needed new office space to handle increased sales in new territories. It all added up to the need for a new building.

The brewery already owned land right across the street on which to construct the new building. John Schorr's family home, the old cooper shop and the former stables would need to be demolished, and the present office building would have to be moved to a different spot, but that didn't represent a big challenge. Architect Robert W. Layer was hired to design the building. His concepts included new company offices, a tap room, new bottling and canning lines and a loading dock capable of handling multiple trucks at the same time. New glass lined stainless steel tanks would be installed in the basement to provide storage capacity for nearly three quarters of a million bottles of beer. By 1949, the building was complete.

This artist's rendition of the new bottling plant was used, among other reasons, to obtain financing to build it. When it was completed, it housed the brewery's offices, the bottling and shipping departments and the new canning equipment. The building stands today and is used as a warehouse.

The main office in the new building is shown in this 1949 photo. At the rear on the right side of the picture is the vault. This office looks the same today as it did in this photo, minus the furniture and the two ladies, Ruth Coburn on the right and the unknown woman on the left.

Between the new building and almost $250,000 in new equipment, the brewery now had nearly $1,000,000 in new debt, something it hadn't had in years. (6/27) In May of that year, Goldcrest 51 Beer became available in 12 oz. conetop cans featuring the company logo on a blue background. (6/28) New brewery branches were established in Kennett, Mo. and Nashville, Tenn. Additional distributors were added in El Dorado, Ark., Paducah, Ky., Cairo, Ill., Jackson, Gulfport, Meridian, Hattiesburg and Canton, Miss.; Cookeville, Tenn. and Sikeston, Mo. (6/29)

Bock beer was never a huge seller in the south. But it did have its fans. Bock beer was aged through the winter and sold in the spring. In 1949, Goldcrest Bock was introduced in 12 and 32 oz. bottles carrying this label. It would only last two years before it would disappear from the shelves forever.

Goldcrest 51 Bock was introduced in both 12 and 32 oz. bottles and promoted with 2500 Bock "hangers," a stock color poster from Gamse Lithography Company of Baltimore, Md. (6/30) The brand would last two years before it disappeared. Three unique neon signs were made to go in the new building's offices, tap room and bottle shop that read "Finest Beer You Ever Tasted." (6/31) It was the brewery's main slogan during the post-war years. All three signs disappeared when the brewery closed and no trace of them has been seen since.

The Tennessee Brewing Company was relatively late in canning its beer. The first can was used in 1935 by the Krueger Brewing Company of New Jersey. It wasn't until 1949 that Goldcrest 51 was sold in this first 12 oz. can. Note the cone shaped top on the can. This type of can was very popular with smaller breweries because they didn't have to buy any new equipment to fill them. Their existing bottling equipment could handle the job with some simple adjustments. But by 1949, the cone top type cans were on their way out to be replaced by flat top cans that could be opened with an opener, commonly called a "church key."

The brewery had three forklifts in its new building's shipping department, each named for one of the three Schorr grandsons, Jake (Jacob B. Schorr, III), Jim (Jim Reardon) and Mike (Mike Reardon). The "Mike" is shown here stacking cases of returnable 12 oz. Goldcrest bottles.

The brewery which had undergone many transformations during its existence, had a "magic" draw that brought people to visit during off hours and provided a pleasant and memorable place to work.

"Papa (brewery secretary John S. Reardon) would take my brother (Mike) and me down to the new bottling plant on Sundays when they weren't working and let us drive the forklifts around," said Jim Reardon, the great grandson of John Schorr. "It was great fun. Each of us had our own forklift, named after us, as did our cousin Jake (Jacob B. Schorr, III)."

Reardon wasn't the only family member to have fond memories of the brewery on Sunday afternoons. "I remember driving the forklifts ...," said J. B. "Jake" Schorr III, a fourth generation descendant of the brewery founder John Schorr. "I also remember getting in the beer boxes and sliding down the conveyors. We had a blast doing that." (6/32)

Sometimes it wasn't all fun and games. Sometimes a little education was incorporated into visits.

"Dad took me down to the brewery many times as a kid," said Fred Dettwiller whose father was E.E. Dettwiller, sales manager for the brewery. "I remember him going through the whole process with me, explaining all the steps in making beer. It was fascinating for a young boy." (6/33)

The fall of 1948 brought this group of Memphis route salesmen, branch managers, distributors and their salesmen to the brewery for a meeting to announce the new building's construction. While at the meeting, they posed for a group picture in front of one of the brewery's transport trucks. Front row (l to r): Joe Coco, Nick Nichols (salesman for Riley Dist., Pine Bluff, Ark.), Jim Nolan, Authur Hightshoe (Helena, Ark. branch manager), unknown, Bob Beard (city sales, Memphis), Bob Brown, Bob Moss (regional sales supervisor), William Bacon (Bacon Dist., Greenville, Miss.), unknown. Back rows (l to r): Jack Barrett, John Riley (Riley Dist., Pine Bluff, Ark.), Homer "Slick" Sharp, Joe Bernadino (city salesman, Memphis), E.E. Dettwiller (brewery sales manager), unknown, unknown, Curtis Nolan, Bill Carter (salesman, Riley Dist., Pine Bluff, Ark.), Frank Tedescucci (Union City, Tenn. branch), Jim Gardner, Pete "Nat" Nickols (city salesman, Memphis), E.C. "Buddy" Krausnick, Jr. (city salesman, Memphis), Huffman Stevenson (Shelbyville, Tenn. branch manager), Vince Coco (Vincent Dist., Little Rock, Ark.), Warren Clark (Dyersburg, Tenn. branch manager), Tony Jetton, Bill Haynes (Jackson, Tenn. branch manager), Ed Bretherick (city salesman, Memphis), Harry Anderson (city sales supervisor, Memphis), unknown, Bill Biggs (brewery assistant sales manager), Hugh Myrick (city salesman, Memphis), unknown.

This group picture was reportedly taken in the tap room of the new offices. The men in the picture were all decked out in their Goldcrest 51 shirts and ties and were mostly Memphis area route salesmen. Front row: (l-r) Ed Brown, Nat Nichols, Ernest Kuehn,Sr., Louis True, Raymond Boggiano. Back rows — Bob Wiggs, Johnny Parr, Jack Richardson, Grossman Dreve, Howard Kirkland, Buddy Krausnick, Joe Norton, unknown, E.E. Dettwiller, Howard Bugg, Ralph James, William McWillie, unknown.

The shortage of metal after the war made signs made from other material more appealing. This sign was made from "Presdwood" a composite material similar to plywood. A paper ad was glued to the presdboard and then coated. It dates from the late 1940s.

This same young man managed to help prevent a problem because he had learned about the bottling process while hanging around.

"One day, I was around where the cases of beer came off a conveyor belt and were loaded on the trucks," he said. "The conveyor belt suddenly came on and cases of beer started appearing and crashing off the end of the belt because there was no one there. I went over and flipped a switch and turned it off. A fellow at the other end of the conveyor came out complaining. He later went to my Dad and said that if I was going to hang around the loading dock I needed a union card. I was 14 at the time so I didn't get one." (6/33)

The equipment was also of interest to at least one Schorr descendant. "I was always fascinated by the mechanical and electrical systems of the brewery," remembered Jake Schorr. "I asked my dad (Jacob B. Schorr, Jr.) lots of

Lighted signs were not something the brewery bought many of, choosing metal and neon as their main type of advertising signs. Only 100 of this 1948 lighted sign were made. This is the only example known to have survived.

The picture is reportedly one of a brewery employee picnic. Several of the brewhouse workers can be identified along with Goldcrest 51 flat top cans which helps place the date of the gathering as 1954.

questions. I guess it helped me later as I was a certified electrician in the Navy in Vietnam." (6/34)

Working in the brewery's new office was also enjoyable. "There was an easy going atmosphere in the office," said Ruth Conerly Meredith who worked in the office from 1948-1951. "We all got along so well. One day, after I had been there a couple of weeks, Mildred Gassaway (the office manager) asked me at lunch if I wanted a beer. It floored me to think about drinking a beer while on the job. It didn't take me long to realize that working in a brewery was different from any other job." (6/35)

Doris Brigance Dolan remembered the company's policy very well. "The brewery was the only place you could work and have a highball or a beer at lunch and no one would say a word to you." (6/36)

Above the main entrance of the new offices built in 1948 is this Goldcrest 51 logo in stone. Hundreds of people, the author of this book included, have tried to figure out how to remove it without tearing up the front of the building. In 1955, before the building was sold, Buddy Krausnick even went so far as to have a contractor give him a price for removing it and repairing the building. The $6000 estimate was a lot of money then. The logo remains intact today.

Ruth Conerly Meredith found the camaraderie of lunchtime enjoyable. "Some of us girls would go down to the tap room and have our lunch. We'd play canasta. It got to be a regular thing." (6/37)

It wasn't just the hourly wage workers who became friends with one another. The brewery employees also found unusual ways to show friendship and a little humor toward the leadership as well.

"On my uncle's (E.E. Dettwiller) 30th birthday, all the route drivers got together and had a parade around his house in their 51 Beer trucks singing

The location of the Main Drive In is unknown but it once promoted 51 Beer with two signs. The neon was a twin to the one shown in Chapter Five. The menu board at the street was probably unique to this restaurant. The brewery made hundreds of these, all customized for the tavern or restaurant in both indoor and outdoor versions.

happy birthday," offered Bill Carter. "It woke him up and I'm sure a few other people in the neighborhood." (6/38)

Brewery employees had one other benefit that no other company offered in 1949 Memphis - free take-home beer. "They gave a case of beer to each employee every week," said Ruth Conerly Meredith. "At the time I had a couple of roommates that didn't care for Goldcrest, so the cases just stacked up. We finally had to have a big party to use it up."

Not only were employees given a case of beer as part of their benefits, the employees were also allowed to take "beer breaks" during the work day. "They brought beer around three times a day," said Richard Campbell who worked in the bottle shop at the brewery during the summer of 1948 between graduating from high school and entering college. "It was in bottles, either shorts or over-filled bottles. I didn't drink myself and at first turned down the free beer. It didn't take long to make friends of the other fellows who wanted my beer." (6/39)

And it wasn't just the employees who enjoyed a free Goldcrest Beer. Hal Newburger's family business occupied the defunct brewery buildings from 1955-1981. "I heard this from lots of the people that stopped by the building over the years," he said. "After 5 o'clock in the afternoon, anybody that

Presenting

Goldcrest 51 BEER

in cans

Ask your dealer today for the Goldcrest 51 Beer that's brewed and fully aged especially for cans. Order 51 Beer in convenient, quick cooling cans. Pack a case of 51 cans for your fishing trip or picnic. Keep 51 cans on hand at home - finest beer you ever tasted.

TENNESSEE BREWING COMPANY
MEMPHIS, TENNESSEE

came by got a free beer. The folks were working people mostly. You had to have your own container, it was right out of the kegs. More than one person remembered how cold the beer was." (6/40)

Others didn't.

"I remember going down to the brewery with my Dad," said former Memphis Director of Police Walter Crews. "We would go down after business hours. He and Mr. (William F. "Wilfred") Ryan (brewery chief engineer) would have a beer and visit. It was fresh beer, right out of the barrel and not very cold. They always talked about how good it was." (6/41)

The beer wasn't the only thing that Walter Crews remembered.

"I had a Daisy Red Rider BB gun that I would take down to the brewery when my Dad took me," he said. "The brewery guys hated the pigeons that roosted on the building. I cer-

When Goldcrest was first canned, this ad appeared in area newspapers announcing the new package. The brewery would only can beer for six years before it closed.

tainly did my part to keep the population down." (6/41)

Pigeons weren't the only creatures that found the brewery attractive. There were sometimes problems with mice in the malt room. One enterprising man thought he might have a solution to keep the mice population under control.

"We had a six-month-old cat we called Tom," reminisced Katherine Kuehn whose husband Ernest Kuehn, Jr. was an engineer at the brewery. "They were having trouble in the malt room with mice, so my husband took the cat in one evening to see if he could catch the mice. At that time we lived about 10 miles from the brewery. The next morning, before Ernie came home from work, the cat was on

The brewery bought thousands of metal tacker signs in the late 1940s and early 1950s from Grace Sign Co. of St. Louis. The small version, shown here, was 22 3/4" x 25". The larger size was 48" x 53 1/4" in the same design. Both sizes came in one and two faced versions and were nailed up on posts and the outside walls of taverns throughout the mid-south. Space for the post with the larger size tacker along area highways was leased for the princely sum of $5 a year.

the back porch of our house. That cat had walked home 10 miles. Ernie said he called and called for Tom at the brewery but he wouldn't come to him. But the mice were still there." (6/42)

There was another aspect to the brewery. It wasn't a place full of vermin as Joe Signagio remembered. "The one thing I remember about the brewery the best was the brew house. It was pristine. Immaculate. You could eat off the floor." (6/43)

Hundreds of these small indoor neons were used by the brewery to promote its flagship brand in taverns. The "circle" neons were made by several different sign companies throughout the mid south but most were made by the Balton Sign Co. of Memphis.

Chapter Seven

*D*espite new buildings, the year 1949 was the beginning of the end for the Tennessee Brewing Company "I first knew that the brewery was in trouble in late 1949," said E.C. "Buddy" Krausnick, Jr. "In 1948 we sold over half the beer in Memphis. In '49, that started to change."

It has long been speculated that there was no one thing that put the brewery, like a lot of other regional brewers of its day, out of business. Higher taxes and the higher cost of labor were certainly factors, as were the increased costs of raw materials. But there were two main culprits, television advertising and increased competition, that can be blamed for the decline of the Tennessee Brewing Company.

In 1949, television was all the rage. People could sit in their homes and watch movies, sports and variety shows. National brewers like Schlitz, Falstaff, Pabst and Anheuser-Busch saw the potential to increase their sales through television advertising. They did so at the expense of the smaller, regional brewers which had trouble competing with national advertising. The national breweries also did not rest on television advertising alone. They and other brewers also increased their aggressive efforts in the local markets.

"I remember when Champagne Velvet came into Memphis for the first time," said E.C. "Buddy" Krausnick, Jr. "They were very aggressive. They hired 30 men for the trade. Their sole job was to go into a tavern and order a 51 Beer.

Annual Report
to
Stockholders

Goldcrest
51
BEER

TENNESSEE BREWING COMPANY
Memphis, Tennessee

YEAR ENDED DECEMBER 31, 1949

After Prohibition, the brewery's stockholders weren't just family members of the three founders. By 1949, the company's stock was owned by several hundred different people and was publicly sold. This annual report covered the year 1949.

After they took a sip, they'd start talking loudly about how green it was. Then they'd order a C.V. and start bragging on its taste. Of course, everything they said was loud enough for everyone in the place to hear. It did what they intended it to do, and it hurt us. We found out what they were doing when we hired three of those fellows and they told us what the C.V. people told them to do. All three said the same thing. In 1948, we had 53 percent of the beer market in Memphis. We owned the beer business here (Memphis). The only way somebody could really hurt us was to start something like that. It was real low of them to do that. It sure wasn't the way we did business." (7/1)

In 1949, the brewery entered the local television advertising market in Memphis. (7/2) Ads aired during boxing on the old Dumont network as well as in the breaks between programs. By 1951, television ads were produced to highlight the new "Extra Aged" ad campaign, featuring the new labels on bottles of 51 Beer. (7/3)

One of the more interesting signs used by the brewery in 1949 was one done in Spanish. The metal sign read "If you want a delicious bottle of Goldcrest 51 Beer — point to this sign."

An evening, reportedly at the Peabody Hotel's famous ballroom, could be best enjoyed with a bottle of Goldcrest Beer, especially for these brewery salesman and their wives. Note that each bottle of beer has its label pointing at the camera for maximum advertising value, a "trick of the trade" taught to them by the brewery management. (l to r) Grossman Dreve, Mamie Dreve, unknown, Pete "Nat" Nickols, Jacob B. Schorr, Sr., unknown, Ed Brown, Doris Brown, unknown.

The piece was used in eastern Arkansas to appeal to migrant farm workers in the area. (7/4) That same year marked the highest number of neons bought by the brewery in any one year. More than 600 indoor neons alone were purchased for use throughout the mid-south. (7/5)

The year 1949 also brought a new marketing push of the flagship brand, known to many area residents as "51" Beer. "My uncle (brewery Sales Manager E.E. Dettwiller) was the one that really pushed to bring out the "51" in the beer's name," said Bill Carter, who worked with one of the brewery's Arkansas distributors. "He was smart enough to recognize that people remembered easy names like Bud instead of Budweiser and pushed the "51" because people would remember it."

Goldcrest in 12 packs of the new 12 oz. cans could now be purchased, as well as new one-way 12 oz. and quart bottles. All the bottled Goldcrest Beer had foil labels for the first time. Many new efforts were being made to get the Goldcrest name in front of the public. A retailer stocking Goldcrest beer would probably be offered a box cutter with the Goldcrest logo on it, while a cafe might have gotten one of 1000 menu boards purchased that year by the brewery. Ladies were invited to write the brewery for a free recipe book entitled "Beer Cookery."

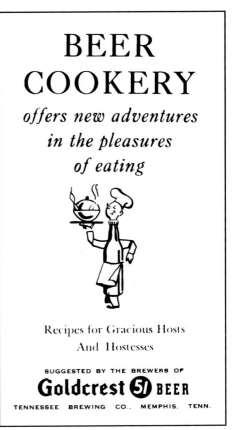

BEER COOKERY

offers new adventures in the pleasures of eating

Recipes for Gracious Hosts And Hostesses

SUGGESTED BY THE BREWERS OF

Goldcrest 51 BEER

TENNESSEE BREWING CO., MEMPHIS, TENN.

One of, if not the last remaining wall sign today was painted in 1949 by Jim Scott on the side of a neighborhood grocery store on the corner of Calhoun and Front streets, not

In the middle part of the 20th Century, beer was primarily bought by the lady of the house at the local grocer when not bought at a tavern. Thus, breweries were always trying to get the attention of the wife. A recipe booklet was given out in 1949 full of recipes that could only contain Goldcrest 51 Beer.

two blocks from the brewery itself. (7/6) "Dad (who painted signs for the brewery beginning in the late 40s and continued until it closed) always referred to himself as being self employed, but the brewery kept him really busy," reminisced Scott's daughter Jane Howell. "He did lots of menu boards with the Goldcrest logo on them. He did lots of wall signs for the brewery, too. He'd point them out when we were in the car." (7/7) The wall signs were a popular form of advertising in the 1940s in the mid-south. Scott painted most of the wall signs for the brewery and painted the beer delivery trucks as well.

When a commercial building was torn down in the early 1990s on Jackson Ave. in Memphis, this painted wall sign was uncovered. Wall signs were very popular forms of advertising for the brewery in the 1940s and 1950s. This one has disappeared again today, this time under a coat of white paint.

"When I was 5 or 6," explained Howell, "we would go down to the brewery on Saturday mornings when the trucks were all in. Dad would paint the trucks, Mom and I would piddle around while he was there. The old building impressed me, it was really scary looking for a young girl." (7/7)

Charles Conerly, an All American quarterback at Ole Miss who later went on to fame with the National Football League's New York Giants, was hired by the brewery as a point man for the state of Mississippi as the year began. It was to be a short relationship. "He was a quiet kind of guy who didn't say much," said Conerly's sister Ruth who also worked for the brewery in the office. "The brewery wanted him to be their public relations guy. He just wasn't cut out for that." By March, Conerly was back helping his father on the family farm. He would later go on to grace the cover of Sports Illustrated magazine in 1956 and be the first "Marlboro Man" in print ads, chosen for the role because of his rugged good looks.

E.C. "Buddy" Krausnick, Jr. remembered a Goldcrest indoor advertising sign of that era that stood out. "It was an electric sign with a bottle of 51 and a glass. Beer was poured from the bottle into the glass. It required water and a powder that you added to the bottle to give the impression of a head on the beer. Problem was you had to recharge the darn thing every 10 days or so because the water would evaporate out. Hopefully, you had a good tavern owner who would call you when the thing needed servicing. Otherwise, you went from a great looking beer to a flat beer with no head pretty quick. That was the most clever sign I ever saw," he said. No example of this sign is known to exist today.

The brewery made several attempts over the years to sell an ale. The last attempt was 51 Ale. It was only packaged in 12 oz. and 32 oz. returnable bottles.

By 1952, ads featured Memphis golfer and dentist Cary Middlecoff who had won the U.S. Open in 1949, would win it again in 1956 and also won the Masters in 1955.

"He was always concerned with his image," said E.C. "Buddy" Krausnick, Jr. "Like all the athletes of that time, Cary did not want to be photographed drinking beer. He said he would do anything else we wanted him to do but that. This is the Bible Belt, you know." Middlecoff would be featured in numerous television ads for 51 Beer in 1952 and 1953. "He was a dentist and a golfer," said Krausnick who was a lifelong friend of Middlecoff's. "I think he was a lot better golfer than he was a dentist."

The company tried to keep up with the competition by using new advertising and new packaging but it was too little, too late. National brewers such as Schlitz, Anheuser-Busch and Falstaff were steadily eating away at the brewery's sales. It wouldn't take long to finish it off.

"It was destined to go," said Joe Signaigo, sales manager for the brewery in 1953. "They couldn't compete with the national brands and their big advertising budgets."

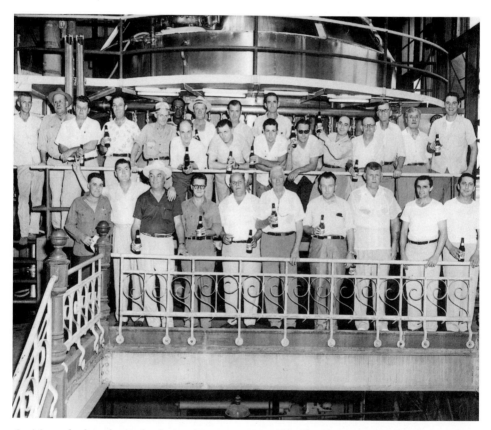

A visit to the brewhouse by former Brewmaster Vollie Schorr June 30, 1953 was a perfect time for a group picture of the men who actually made Goldcrest Beer. The brewhouse workers gathered, complete with a presumably cold Goldcrest Beer in front of the 365 barrel brew kettle. Most of the names of these men are unknown but some can be identified. On the front row, fourth from the left is E.B. Kuehn, Jr.. To his right is J.B. Schorr, Jr.. Next to him is Vollie Schorr. At the far right of the front row is Henry Loenneke. On the top row, the third man from the left is Wilford Ryan. The names of the others are unknown.

*A*s the 1950s opened, the brewery had more challenges than ever before. Aside from the declining profits due to the increased competition of the national brewers and the additional debt from the new bottling plant and offices, the brewery was losing most of its key people. By the summer of 1952, all of the head positions with the company would change. John Reardon, company secretary, left in May 1950 and was replaced by C.C. Starnes (8/1). E.E. Dettwiller, sales manager, left in July of 1951 to go to Nashville, Tenn. as the distributor for Sterling Beer. (8/2)

"It wasn't his first chance to go out on his own," said Dettwiller's son Fred. "He had at least one other opportunity in Memphis but he felt it would be disloyal to compete head to head with the brewery." (8/3)

E.C. "Collie" Krausnick was the brewery's first vice president when he passed away Jan. 3, 1952. He was the grandson of Caspar Koehler, one of the founders of the brewery and represented Koehler's decendants who owned a huge block of the company's stock. He was well liked and was said to actually be the day-to-day manager of the brewery at the time of his death.

First vice-president E. Carl "Collie" Krausnick, Sr. passed away Jan. 3, 1952 from heart failure (8/4) and C.C. Starnes was promoted to his position. Krausnick's son, E.C. "Buddy" Krausnick, Jr. was promoted to the secretary position. (8/5) Jacob Schorr then resigned as president in August 1952 and assumed the new title of chairman of the board. (8/6) C.C. Starnes was appointed president and treasurer and E.C. "Buddy" Krausnick, Jr. was appointed vice president and secretary. (8/7) The changes were not over in 1952. Starnes resigned in August 1953. (8/8) The last lineup of company officers went in place in September 1953. E.C. "Buddy" Krausnick, Jr. was president; J.B. Schorr, Jr. was appointed vice president/production; B. Frank Jenkins was appointed vice president/sales; W. C. McWillie was named treasurer; Joe Signaigo, a former All American football player at Notre Dame, was appointed sales manager; (8/9) and J.O.E. Beck, a large stockholder in the company was chairman of the board. E.C. "Buddy" Krausnick, Jr. was the great grandson of Caspar Koehler, one of the founders of the brewery.

The grandson of one of the brewery's founders, John W. Schorr, John Schorr Reardon was the secretary of the brewery until 1950. He grew up in John Schorr's home next to the brewery and as a child accompanied his grandparents all over the country and to Canada during the thoroughbred racing seasons.

John Reardon, corporate secretary until 1950, was perhaps the most colorful of all the people who worked at the brewery. His likable personality, combined with a zest for living made him one of the brewery people who really stood out. He inherited all his grandfather John Schorr's stock in the company through his mother, Gertrude Anne Schorr Reardon, as her only child. She had inherited the stock in much the same way as the only child of Rachel Schorr, the second wife of John Schorr. Reardon sold all his stock after leaving the company and took his family on a vacation that lasted more than two years. While on this trip, the family stayed in the finest hotels and lived a life of luxury.

"When he sold his stock in the family business a lot of people chastised him," said Bill Carter. "When the brewery went out of business 4 to 5 years later, he had the last laugh. He said he always wanted to live like a millionaire and he did for a couple of years after he left the brewery." (8/10)

"My Dad (E.E. Dettwiller) and John Reardon (grandson of John Schorr and brewery secretary) were good friends," said Fred Dettwiller. "On my eighth birthday, John Reardon came down our street leading a pony. He decided that I needed a pony for my birthday present. Now

Reportedly, the 51 cake was for E.E. Dettwiiller's 30th birthday. Pictured with Dettwiller, the brewery's sales manager is Bill Haynes, the manager of the brewery's Jackson, Tenn. branch.

These two 32 oz. cans represent the only attempts the brewery made to can more than 12 ounces at a time. The one on the left was first used in 1950 and the one on the right was introduced in March 1952. This size can was popular with minority consumers yet represented a very small percentage of the brewery's output. Neither of the quart cans have many examples that exist today and almost all that do are in poor shape. The two shown are among, if not the best, known examples today.

Introduced in May 1951, the character Mr. 51 promoted Goldcrest 51 Beer. This 5 1/2" pilsner glass was passed out by the hundreds to taverns and bars in the brewery's trade area. The glass is the only item of a few things produced with Mr. 51 that remains in any quantity today in collections.

In an effort to maintain a lower priced package for Goldcrest Beer, the brewery introduced a 7 oz. bottle in 1951 called a "split." Two different labels were used, one modeled after the "premium" can label and the other a "select" label. It was thought that the smaller package would also appeal to women drinkers. The size was marketed for less than three years. This metal sign is one of the more common pieces in collections. It was purchased by the brewery for 82 cents in June 1951.

you can imagine he attracted quite a crowd of kids walking down that street with a pony. I was scared. I had never had a pony before and didn't know how to care for one. The pony was sent to my uncle and aunt's farm the next day. Reardon was a real character." (8/11)

While the handwriting may have been on the wall, the brewery didn't stop its efforts to survive and improve its product presentation. Quart cans were introduced in April 1950. (8/12) New 7 oz. returnable bottles, called "splits" hit the shelves in the spring of 1951.

"When we introduced the 7 oz. splits bottle, we bought hundreds of orchids," reminisced E.C. "Buddy" Krausnick, Jr. "The route men gave an orchid to the wife or girlfriend of the store or tavern owner. We ordered more orchids than we had customers, which turned out to be a good thing. We had customers calling the brewery for days asking for more orchids and more beer. We sold a lot of beer because of those flowers."

Goldcrest 51 Beer was introduced in Nashville, Tenn. in 1951. This newspaper ad appeared to herald the news. The branch office in Nashville lasted less than two years.

A new advertising character was introduced in May 1951, a man with a gay 90s look wearing a bowler hat, Mr. 51. (8/13) He appeared in newspaper ads, billboards, fiber boxes for returnable bottles, cardboard signs, one lighted sign (8/14) and on two sizes of glasses, a 5 1/2" pilsner and a 3 1/2" barrel. Metal display racks were ordered for the first time as were mirrored glass signs. Tacker signs continued to be a major source of advertising support, including a new "Splits" tacker advertising the new 7 oz. bottles at a

TENNESSEE BREWING CO., MEMPHIS, TENN.

Goldcrest was proclaimed the "Beer of the Year" for 1951 in this newspaper ad which featured the brewery's two main packages, the 12 oz. returnable bottle and 12 oz. can. Note that the name "Goldcrest" is not mentioned in the copy of this ad, only the more common name "51" was promoted.

When Goldcrest 51 Select was introduced in March 1952, postcards like this example were mailed out to merchants thoughout the brewery's trade area. Most were sent with a local radio station listed that carried programs or advertisements that the brewery or its distributors sponsored and when they could be heard.

The addition of the Select brand name meant a change in the packaging for Goldcrest Beer, including this revised 12 oz. conetop can. The white background was painted with very thin paint. Thus, almost all the specimens that have survived are in rough condition. This can was only used in 1952.

price of 10 cents. (8/15) A new brewery branch was opened in Tennessee's second largest city and was initially successful. "The company opened a branch office in Nashville," said Bill Carter. "They promoted it heavily and were selling a lot of beer. The people in Nashville loved 51 Beer. So the management decided to stop spending money on advertising in the Nashville mar-

One of the oddest items that was produced by or for the brewery was this tool which has the Select logo. Its actual function is unknown but it stands to reason that it was made for workers in the bottling department of the brewery because of its various grips and opener.

ket. Sales went sour in a hurry. The branch was closed within a year." (8/16)

Work began in late 1950 to improve the taste and image of Goldcrest 51. A way was also sought to reduce the amount of time spent aging the new product. This would help increase sales without additional storage space being necessary. In March 1952, Goldcrest 51 Select was introduced. (8/17) The idea originated with the brewery's advertising agency, Westheimer and Block of Saint Louis which had used the "Select" name with other regional brewers. The advertising budget for 1952 was set at $1.50 per barrel to introduce the new brand, a figure that was among the highest in the industry. (8/18)

In a preview of what Coca-Cola learned with its introduction of New Coke in the 1980s, the new product replaced the flagship brand and the result was disastrous. Sales continued to slide and Goldcrest 51 Premium came back to the retailer's shelves right after the first of 1953. Very few advertising pieces were made to support the Select brand during its short history. A couple of 3' x 5' metal signs

Two sizes of this Goldcrest 51 Select sign were produced. This is the larger one (48"x 53 1/4"). The smaller version (22 3/4" x 25") is an exact replica of the larger sign. The brewery did not spend a lot on signs for the Select brand and little of what they did survives today.

are known to have survived and some letterhead, company checks and fiber boxes for returnable bottles show the Select name. Display cards in both English and Spanish were printed for the "Selecta" brand. (8/19) Additionally, a mirrored glass sign and an acetate sign were ordered, as was a "pretty girl display piece." (8/20) Quart size and 12 oz. conetop cans were produced for the Select brand as were 7, 12 and 32 oz. bottles. For the first and only time, a 16 oz. bottle was also used. (8/21)

Whether times were tough or not, there were people who appreciated the beer and the atmosphere of the Tennessee Brewing Company. Even a group of Germans, who without a doubt can be the most discerning when it comes to beer, found Goldcrest to be more than acceptable.

"In 1951, there were a group of German business people touring around various companies in Memphis," said E.C. "Buddy" Krausnick, Jr. the last president of the brewery. "We got a call from the Chamber (of Commerce) people asking if we'd entertain them and feed them lunch. We had sandwiches and the like brought in and served them lunch in our tap room. Being as they were Germans, I brought in

This was the second can made by the brewery, a 12 oz. variation of the first can which removed the company logo of the man sitting on a cotton bale and replaced it with the word "premium." This can was introduced in early 1950 along with its quart size cousin and has two variations stemming from small differences in the label.

This 36" wide oval sign was used during the last few years of the brewery's existence. This particular sign was actually part of an order that was being filled when the brewery closed. The author found a sign company in Little Rock which ended up having 12 of them in storage in 1993.

an accordion player to play for them. I had to go to the office for a while and left them with the food, the accordion player and the taps of beer. After a while, they were all singing and drinking and having a grand time. They were supposed to leave us at 1:30 and tour the Plough Pharmaceuticals plant. They never got there. Thank goodness they were all on the same bus and didn't have to drive themselves back to their hotel because there wasn't a one of them walking a straight line." (8/22)

Although Goldcrest was still being enjoyed by many, the fight was almost over. By 1953 sales had slipped to just 67,410 barrels and the company lost $291,458. (8/23) Desperate times forced desperate measures. An attempt was made to sell the brewery to other brewers. Chairman August "Gussie" Busch of Anheuser-Busch expressed interest and sent a team to Memphis to inspect the brewery and report its findings directly to him.

"I went to St. Louis and met with Gussie," said E.C. "Buddy" Krausnick, Jr. "He was particularly interested in us because of our new building and equipment. I told him that we'd sell him the brewery, including the new building and canning line for less than a million dollars. He'd get a $900,000 tax loss, too. His inspection team even left here saying they would suggest to "Gussie" that he buy us but something happened after they went back that changed his mind. It's

E.C. "Buddy" Krausnick, Jr. was the last president of the brewery. After the brewery closed, he went into the insurance business in Memphis where he still resides. This picture is from March, 2003.

This sign was used by the brewery in 1951 to appeal to minority consumers. The sign is die cut, on an easel with a self hanger tab and its size is 19 1/2" X 15". This was one of the few signs the brewery produced aimed at minorities. Most of the minority advertising done by the brewery was in the form of radio ads and short films shown at theatres.

a shame because that would have been a good deal for both of us."

Anheuser-Busch passed on the Memphis brewery and eventually purchased the American Brewing Company in Miami, Fla.

In a different tact to stay alive, the brewery sold some additional stock in 1953. "The company had a preferred stock sale to raise money for operating capital," said Joe Signaigo, the brewery's sales manager then. "Most everyone in the brewery, myself included, bought some."

Another attempt to shore up flagging sales resulted in a sales promotion in 1953 which sounds extremely similar to soft drink promotions used today.

"Approximately 1 of every 200 bottles had a yellow "51" logo stamped

Note the outfield fence at Memphis' Russwood Park on the left side. The 1952 season saw a Goldcrest Select ad on the fence. Outfield fence ads were used by the brewery to promote its beer beginning before Prohibition. You could see a Goldcrest ad on the fence in ballparks all over the mid-south in the 1950s. *Photo courtesy of the Memphis/Shelby County Public Library and Information Center.*

This store display is from a Memphis grocer in early 1950. Note that the top shelf contains both versions of the 12 oz. blue can sold for only 16 cents each. Goldcrest 51 was sold at that time in returnable 12 and 32 oz. bottles, one way 12 and 32 oz. bottles and 12 oz. cans. This photo illustrates some of the competitors on the other shelves that would play a big role in the brewery closing in 1954.

on the back of the label. If you got that label, your next 51 was free," said E.C. "Buddy" Krausnick, Jr. "The retailers really liked that one because they used up more beer."

On January 30, 1954 the brewery signed an agreement with Glazer Wholesale Drug Company of Dallas, Tex. to contract brew Berghoff 1887 Beer, a brand that Glazer had the rights to in Texas, Arkansas and Louisiana. (8/24) The brewery also introduced DeSoto Beer, its own brand, for distribution by Glazer in those same states. Neither brand was ever bottled, but each had one 12 oz. can from the brewery's new flat-top canning line.

"We were in trouble," said E.C. "Buddy" Krausnick, Jr. "We weren't

The Berghoff Beer brand was originally made by the Berghoff Brewing Corp. of Ft. Wayne, Ind. By 1954, that brewery had closed and the brand name was sold to several different groups, each purchasing the rights for certian areas of the country. The Tennessee Brewing Co. was contracted to can Berghoff beer for distribution in Arkansas, Louisiana and Texas which made it one of the first contract breweries. This brand was only sold for a few months in 1954.

The last Goldcrest 51 can made by the brewery and the only flat top Goldcrest can, was introduced in early 1954.

Talk about a short-lived brand, the DeSoto brand was introduced in early summer 1954 a few months before the brewery closed. The brand was only canned in this 12 oz. version and was sold at a popular beer price level. In July 1954, a case of DeSoto cost $4.25. Once the brewery announced it was closing, traincar loads of DeSoto and Goldcrest were sold all over the country at discount prices. Examples of DeSoto have been unearthed in dumps from California to Georgia. Its metallic blue background does not mesh well with the humidity of the south so most examples of this can today are much less than pristine.

selling enough beer to keep our men working so we started those brands up. We had a contract with the union (Brewery Worker's Local #196), eight hours a day, 40 hours a week. We needed something other than 51 to keep them working. We didn't make any money on either brand. We priced it at a break even price. It was a brokerage beer, today they'd call it a contract beer. It was the same beer, whether it came in a 51 bottle or a Berghoff or DeSoto can. Exact same beer."

Neither of the new brands was ever sold in Memphis but they were sold in some new, distant places for the company's beer. Shipping records reflect how desperate the company had become to sell beer. In the summer of 1954, Goldcrest 51 was sold to distributors in Augusta, Ga., Omaha, Neb., Los Angeles, Calif., and Orlando and Tampa, Fla. Berghoff was sent to Glazer's warehouses all over Texas, Little Rock, Ark. and New Orleans, La. DeSoto had the widest distribution of the brewery's brands. Aside from Glazer's warehouses, it was shipped to San Jose, Calif., Los Angeles, Calif., Hollywood, Calif., Augusta, Ga., Jacksonville and Orlando, Fla., Omaha, Neb. and all the company's distributors in Alabama. (8/25) No advertising exists for either the Berghoff or DeSoto brand and the cans are highly prized by collectors.

An article in the Memphis Press-Scimitar September 16, 1954 announced to the public that the end was in sight. "The last shipment of Memphis made beer will be sent out in about two weeks. Company trucks will make Memphis deliveries of Goldcrest 51 for the last time tomorrow (9/17/54)." It came as no great surprise to many people, especially those who worked at the brewery.

"I left before that because I had a good opportunity to own my own business," said Ed Bretherick. "Besides, we all knew the brewery was about to close." (9/1) Brewmaster J.B. Schorr, Jr. reportedly had even tried to mortgage his home to raise money for the failing brewery but his wife Mildred refused. (9/2)

But Bretherick had good memories of the work he did for the brewery while he was an employee there from 1945-54 and he remembered how well Goldcrest Beer sold in Mississippi during its heyday.

"The brewery sent me down to Mississippi to solicit bootleggers and the like," he said. "These areas I went in to were dry back then (late 40s). I remember working all the cafes in Yazoo City and got 100 per cent distribution. The distributor in the next county, which was wet, never officially sold a case of our beer in Yazoo City but he sure made some good money off those cafes. In Sunflower County, I worked all the joints. The county was dry but they all sold beer freely. Beer in the front room, poker and dice in the back. That's the way it was back then. The owner of the joint would sign for the beer he wanted, send a truck up to Memphis and we'd load him up with Goldcrest Beer." (9/3)

The heydey of Goldcrest beer in the 40s was

This sterling silver opener was made for the board room at the brewery and is the only one known.

on a fast decline by the early 50s and according to at least one former employee, national advertising and stockholders concern for a profit were two of the reasons.

"The big boys really overwhelmed them with advertising," said Bill Carter, who worked with one of the brewery's Arkansas distributors. "Plus, they had a bunch of stockholders who were more interested in dividends than operating the business profitably. Let me give you an example. Around 1950, the company sold off all its rolling stock. All its transport trucks, trailers, route trucks, everything. Sold it all to Hertz and then turned around and leased it all right back from them. Why? To raise cash so that they could pay a dividend to the stockholders. They sold off an asset just to pay a dividend."

The end of the brewery didn't mean the end of the beer business for Bill Carter, who got involved in the Memphis brewery because of a relative.

"My uncle, E.E. Dettwiller, was the sales manager for the brewery," he said. "He came to me and asked me if I would like to work in the beer business. At the time, I was working for $48.50 a week and my wife was pregnant. He offered me $50.00 a week and I needed that $1.50. So I moved to Pine Bluff, Ark. (to work for

This large patch was made to adorn the back of a jacket. Smaller patches were made for the front of jackets and shirts. Several styles of patches were made over the years.

Goldcrest Distributor Riley Distributing) and got into the beer business. Been in it ever since." (9/4)

Family connections were often used to find jobs in the brewery.

"I got my job at the brewery through my now wife's grandfather, August Rinn," recalled Richard Campbell. "He was one of the founders of the union at the brewery. He started there in 1890 and retired in 1944. He

Matchbooks were an inexpensive form of advertising in the 1950s when a large percentage of Americans smoked. Breweries used them a lot, although this is the only one known from the Tennessee Brewing Co.

always talked about making beer at the brewery, about being one of the brewmasters. He and Vollie Schorr, after they both retired, would sit and reminisce about the brewery for hours. The thing I remember about that best is the fact that they'd finish each other's sentences. They knew each other so well." (9/5)

The leadership of the brewery wasn't finished trying to ease the financial difficulties. It wanted to get to the bottom of the decline in sales and set out to do just that in the early 50s.

"In the fall of 1951, my Dad (E.C. "Collie" Krausnick) decided that we were going to get a better handle on why our sales were down," said E.C. "Buddy" Krausnick, Jr. "We knew that we were putting out a good product, so we had a taste test promotion at local bars. We'd go in the bar and when we saw someone order a beer other than '51', we'd ask them if we could buy them two beers, a '51' and their choice of beer. We wrapped them up in brown paper bags and poured the beers into unmarked glasses. Out of over 1,600 people we did this with, the results were almost an identical number for '51' and their choice of beer. Taste wasn't the reason they were ordering other brands. The main reason was all the advertising the other guys were doing. Our best year, we made over 200,000 barrels of beer. Anheuser-Busch made over 5 million barrels a year in the early 50s. They had the money to advertise, we didn't. That's what did us in." (9/6)

Closing meant an end to the financial bleeding that the company had endured for years. During December 1953, only 3,797 barrels were brewed representing just 11 batches of beer in the company's 350 barrel brew kettle. (9/7) It hadn't gotten any better by the summer of 1954. The officers of the company met in late July, made the decision to close and a shareholders meeting was quickly scheduled. "Things got a little heated at that meeting," said E.C. "Buddy" Krausnick, Jr. "I even had to ask the sergeant at arms to

This is the bottling department in 1908 when 1,250 units an hour could be filled between the three bottling machines in operation like the one shown. Tom Doyle (third from right, foreground) was a filling machine operator. Julius Kuehn (far right) operated the crowning machine. *Photo courtesy of the Commercial Appeal.*

Tom Doyle (left) and Julius Kuehn (right) worked for the brewery in the bottling department beginning before Prohibition. They were still there when the brewery closed in 1954. This picture was taken mere days before the brewery closed. *Photo courtesy of the Commercial Appeal.*

Here's how the brewery looked a few days before it closed. The shipping area in the back of the new bottling building is on the right. The 1890 buildings in the center of the photo were used for the manufacture and aging of beer. When the brewery closed in 1954 it had sold most of its delivery trucks. Those shown here were probably leased. *Photo courtesy of the Commercial Appeal.*

escort one stockholder out of the room who was using language that wasn't appropriate."

The stockholders were mostly Memphians, including Krausnick himself. "If I had known then what I know now, I'd have closed the brewery sooner," said Krausnick. "I personally lost thousands of dollars in stock value alone." (9/8)

The brewery's employees were notified on September 10, 1954 that the company was closing. "This is to notify you Friday, Sept. 17 will terminate your employment at the Tennessee Brewing Company" was how the letter began. (9/9) Julius J. "Pop" Kuehn who had been at the brewery longer than anyone else, 54 years, was quoted in the Commercial Appeal as saying that the closing was "like losing my home." He was not the only one that left the brewery unhappy.

Some were sad because it was the end of an era. More were sad because

This view looks west down Butler Ave. in the late summer of 1954, with the brewery offices on the left. Note the older buildings at the end of the street (center right). These are the original buildings of the old Memphis Brewing Co. The exact date of their demolition is unknown but it was in 1963. *Photo courtesy of the Commercial Appeal.*

In this recent photo, you can see the 1890 buildings looming in the background behind the 1949 bottling plant. John W. Schorr's home sat on the same spot as the general office part of the building on the left. While the future of these buildings remains unknown, owners who now have control say they want to preserve them. That is probably the best hope for them.

The corporate logo featured a man sitting on a cotton bale. The brewery rarely used the logo after Prohibition and never prominently. The origin of the logo is a mystery.

it meant that they didn't have a job. "I got word that the brewery would close and I asked the sales supervisors in and told them," said Joe Signaigo. "I was young and wasn't worried about another job but a lot of them weren't. It was a sad day for a lot of people." (9/10) Two hundred employees would feel the ax.

"I remember my mother and I picking up Daddy at the loading docks after work," said Charlotte Clark whose father was Grossman Dreve a route salesman in the late 40s and 50s. "If the brewery were open today and he was alive he would still be working there." (9/11)

Doris Brigance Dolan who worked in the brewery office said, "I worked at the brewery until the end of November 1954. It was a chore to be there knowing what was coming up." (9/12) On September 24, the brewery sold the last remaining beer it had in its cellars. (9/13)

Prior to the time when the brewery was closing, Dolan, who began work there in 1945 remembered some of the good natured interaction between employees, especially with E.C. "Collie" Krausnick.

"Ruth Tutt (who worked in the brewery office) and I went to Cuba in 1950 for a vacation," she remembered. "Mr. (Collie) Krausnick called us in his office before we left to give us some pointers. He said that if you want to meet a rich man not to hang out in the hotel bar but to get a cabana next to the pool. We rented a cabana, as he had suggested, but nothing happened. We ended up in the bar and that's where we found all the guys. When we returned we told Mr. Krausnick that he had given us some bad information. He didn't say anything, he just smiled." (9/14)

The final process of selling off the brewery fell to good-natured E.C. "Buddy" Krausnick, Jr. and company Treasurer W.C. McWillie. "We had tried to sell the whole brewery several times but it just didn't come together," said Krausnick. "So, we set out in '55 to sell it one piece at a time." (9/15)

Equipment was sold to numerous breweries including Anheuser-Busch, Jax Brewing Company (Jacksonville, Fla.), Queen City Brewing Company (Cumberland, Md.), Monarch Brewing Company (Chicago), C. Schmidt Brewing Company (Philadelphia, Pa.), Adam Scheidt Brewing Company (Philadelphia, Pa.), Arizona Brewing Company (Phoenix), Virginia Brewing Company (Roanoke), Fisher Brewing Company (Salt Lake City) and others. (9/16)

Wooden aging tanks were sold to a pickle manufacturer in Oklahoma. (9/17) Perhaps, aside from its buildings, the brewery's most valuable possession was the trademark on the name Goldcrest 51 Beer. The rights to the name were sold to the Atlantic Brewing Company of Chicago until July 1, 1955 when it would revert back to Tennessee Brewing Company. Atlantic Brewing paid royalties on all sales of Goldcrest 51 in selected southern states but paid no royalties outside those states. (9/18) Atlantic Brewing, through its subsidiary Lederer Brewing Company sold Goldcrest 51 in both cans and bottles using the same designs as the Tennessee Brewing Company had. In February, 1955, the brewery sold the rights to the tradename "DeSoto Beer" to a James A. Martin, Jr. of Biloxi, Miss. for $700.00. The sales price included all the art, designs and printing dyes for the 12 oz. DeSoto can and 6-pack holder. No royalties were to be collected on DeSoto sales by the brewery. There is no evidence that Martin ever produced beer under the DeSoto tradename or sold the name to anyone else who produced beer under this name.

By the summer of 1955, most of the equipment, barrels and tanks that had value had been sold. The Atlantic Brewing Company decided to pass on renewing its ownership of the tradename Goldcrest 51 Beer and it too was sold to James Martin on June 24, 1955. (9/19) Martin paid $1000.00 plus a royalty of two cents per case up to an annual maximum of $4000.00. The Queen City Brewing Company also canned Goldcrest 51 Beer leading to speculation that Martin sold the rights to them, although that has not been documented. Queen City also produced Goldcrest 51 in both cans and bottles initially using the same design as Tennessee Brewing had.

The original brewery buildings, including those purchased from the Memphis Brewing Company in 1885 and the adjacent 1890 buildings, were sold September 13, 1955 to A. Karchmer & Son, a Memphis scrap metal dealer, for $66,000. (9/20) It would occupy the buildings until 1981. "We bought the building for two reasons," offered Hal Newburger of Karchmer & Son. "One, to use it as our office and the courtyard to store metals. Second, as a scrap metals dealer, the building was full of pipes and tanks." (9/21) The original Memphis Brewing Company buildings would be torn down in 1963. (9/22) Today, the spot they were on is a graveled empty lot.

The new bottling plant which had cost nearly $750,000 to build was sold January 20, 1956 to Max Pinkerton and Mark Townsend for $266,250. (9/23) There was not much left to sell. The officials for the brewery notified the Internal Revenue Service that they wished to cease all operations April 1, 1956. Their request was approved. (9/24) "I was the last one to lock the door on the building," reminisced E.C. "Buddy" Krausnick, Jr. "It was kind of sad." (9/25)

This ad appeared in both Memphis area newspapers and industry publications. It would take a year and a half to liquidate everything.

"The thing I remember most about the brewery?" asked Mary Lou Gaerig whose father was "Wilfred" Ryan an engineer at the brewery from 1944-54. "The smell when they made the beer. It's stuck with me all these years." (E/1)

Once the brewery, and the smells of hops and yeast emanating from its buildings ceased to exist, the buildings themselves were turned from brewing to other uses.

The main brewery build was sold to A. Karchmer and Sons Scrap Metal in 1955 and was used by them until 1981. Hal Newburger whose family owns the business said that many people were drawn to the building even after its brewing days were past. People visited, for some reason still drawn to the brick buildings on Tennessee Street.

"There was hardly a week that went by that someone didn't stop by the building and reminisce about the brewery," said Hal Newburger. "People that worked there, people that had dealings with the brewery. It had a special place in a lot of peoples' lives. There is such a personality in that building. You know the old saying that if the walls could talk? Well, I'd love to be there if they started." (E/2)

Since 1981 there has been no permanent occupant, although it has served a Memphis theatre group as a locale for staging plays and in 1992 was used as a location for the movie "Trespass."

The new bottling plant (built in 1949) was sold in January of 1956 to two local investors. Since then it has been used as a mail annex for the U.S. Postal Service and as a warehouse by Royal Furniture Company. It continues as a storage facility today.

The Butler Street Market, a weekend flea market and food outlet, uses the former bottling plant's loading dock and lot.

Some local businessmen even took a stab at reviving the Goldcrest Beer name in the mid 1990s and marketed a Goldcrest 61 beer for a short time. However, they did it without the original recipe.

The recipe was thought to be lost when the company closed its doors in 1954. Jake Schorr said, "I asked my dad (Jacob B. Schorr, Jr. the brewery's last brewmaster) once about the the recipe, but he never would give it to me. He told me that I didn't need to have it. I had the presence of mind to ask, but I didn't pursue it."

The recipe was not known to exist for many years and just recently resurfaced. While researching the book, the author interviewed the child of one of the brew house workers. The son found in the papers of his deceased father what is believed to be the hand-written recipe and instructions for brewing the original Goldcrest 51 beer.

The future of the remaining structures of the Tennessee Brewing Company is yet to be determined. Every day that passes, someone new discovers the brewery buildings for the first time and falls in love with them. One such person is current owner Kevin Norman, who bought the 1890 brewhouse building in 1999. "Ask me why I bought the building and I can't give you a good fiscally sound answer. I just fell in love with it and thought I could save it. The buildings' future remains a bit hazy at best. Using it as art space is the leading candidate right now. It's going to have to ultimately be some sort of mixed use space. I think the brewery could be a fun place to be for coffee shops, art galleries and the like."

In some ways, it's a wonder that the buildings remain today. "In reality, the development community didn't want the building. There's no easy solution to using it," added Norman. "The building's sheer beauty is what attracted me. I can't tell you how many people have fallen in love with this place, many of then who've only driven by it and never seen the inside. Its strength will carry it in the future." (E/3)

So perhaps the buildings on Tennessee Street no longer are used for brewing beer and Goldcrest 51 hasn't been made in almost 50 years, but the Tennessee Brewing Company and its buildings haven't faded away. Perhaps the massive, red brick buildings close to the banks of the Mississippi may even see a revival some day. Neighboring warehouse space has been turned into loft apartments, and empty lots in the area have been filled with new homes. It is believed that the brewery has a place in the future. It certainly has had a impact on the people of Memphis in the past.

SOURCES

Chapter 1

1. American Breweries II, by Dale P. Van Wieren
2. Article, Memphis Daily Appeal, 1/28/1875
3. Schades' Brewers Handbook for 1876
4. Article, Memphis Daily Appeal, 6/2/1877
5. Article, Memphis Daily Appeal, 9/11/1877
6. Article, Memphis Daily Appeal, 4/25/1881
7. Warranty Deed to property, 1/22/1885
8. Contract, 3/22/1885
9. Interview with Buddy Krausnick, 1/20/2002
10. Article, Memphis Daily Appeal, 1/22/1885
11. Article, Memphis Daily Appeal, 5/30/1885
12. Article, Memphis Daily Avalanche, 5/31/1885
13. Article, Memphis Daily Appeal, 6/7/1885
14. Article, Memphis Daily Appeal, 6/7/1885
15. Article, Memphis Daily Appeal, 5/30/1885
16. Interview with Mary Lou Ryan Gaerig, 7/30/2002
17. Article, Memphis Daily Appeal, 8/11/1888
18. Warranty deed on property, 4/27/1891
19. Corporate tax return for 1892
20. Ad, Memphis Appeal-Avalanche, 8/30/1891
21. Ad, Memphis Appeal-Avalanche, 8/30/1891
22. Paul R. Coppock's Mid-South- Vol. II
23. Past Times, Stories of Early Memphis, Pere Magness
24. Article, Memphis Commercial Appeal, 1/9/1930
25. Brewers Journal, April 1895
26. Brewers Journal, 3/18/1898
27. Western Brewer, 12/18/1899
28. Paul R. Coppock's Mid-South- Vol. II
29. United Labor Journal for the year 1900
30. Income Tax return for 1900
31. Paul R. Coppock's Mid-South- Vol. II
32. R.L. Polk's City Directory, 1902
33. Dow's Memphis Directory for 1888
34. Article, Memphis Commercial Appeal, 12/20/1956
35. Article, Housewarming Edition of the Memphis Evening Scimitar for 1903
36. Article, oaklawn.com/history, 2/24/1905
37. Paul R. Coppock's Mid-South- Vol. II
38. Article, Memphis Commercial Appeal, 1/28/1907
39. The Brewer's Handbook for 1906
40. American Brewer's Review, Vol. 21

41. The Brewer's Journal, Vol. 34, Sept. 1910
42. American Brewer's Review, Vol. 23, June 1909
43. Brewers Journal, September, 1906
44. Paul R. Coppock's Mid-South- Vol. II
45. Corporate tax return for 1908
46. Article, Memphis Commercial Appeal, 5/21/1908
47. Ad, Memphis Commercial Appeal, 8/21/1909
48. Prohibition and Politics: Turbulent Decades in Tennessee, 1885-1920, Paul E. Isaac

Chapter 2

1. Article, Memphis Commercial Appeal, 2/27/1917
2. R.L. Polk's Memphis Directory for 1916
3. Article, Memphis Commercial Appeal, 2/27/1917
4. Article, Memphis Commercial Appeal, 2/27/1917
5. Letter from Jacob B. Schorr to Leo Rassieur (corporate director), 3/29/1918
6. Ad, El Paso Herald, 7/13/1920
7. Income tax return for 1926
8. Brewery payroll records, 5/15/1926
9. Letter to brewery from Canadian Dry Ginger Ale Co., 2/25/1929
10. Article, Memphis Commercial Appeal, 1/9/1930
11. Interview with Buddy Krausnick, 1/20/2002
12. Interview with Jim Reardon, 1/20/2002

Chapter 3

1. Interview with Buddy Krausnick, 1/20/2002
2. Article, Memphis Evening Appeal, 5/7/1933
3. Western Brewer, May 1933
4. Article, Memphis Commercial Appeal, 6/16/1933
5. Interview with Eleanor Kuehn Scott, 4/10/2002
6. United States Beer Cans, Beer Can Collectors of America
7. Letter from brewery to Woodward & Tiernan Printing, St. Louis, 11/2/1934
8. Interview with Buddy Krausnick, 1/20/2002
9. Letter from Woodward & Tiernan Printing Co., St. Louis, 2/25/1935
10. Letter from brewery to Woodward & Tiernan Printing Co., St. Louis, 3/4/1935
11. Letter from E.C. Krausnick to Leo Rassieur, 11/19/1935
12. Article, Memphis Commercial Appeal, 4/24/1935
13. Letter to Jacob B. Schorr from Aurther Kammerer (corporate Director), 8/22/1935
14. Letter from Jacob B. Schorr to A.E. Kammerer, 10/4/1935

15. Letter from brewery to Woodward & Tiernan Printing Co., St. Louis, 9/9/1935
16. Telegram to Progress Sign Co., Cincinnati, 2/20/1935
17. Article, Memphis Commercial Appeal, 5/17/1936
18. Paul R. Coppock's Mid-South- Vol. II
19. Article, Memphis Commercial Appeal, 5/17/1936
20. Invoices from Yellow Cab Co. between 3/15/35 and 5/1/1947
21. Letter from John Reardon to Michael Schorr of American Brewing Co. (New Orleans), 12/20/1948
22. Modern Brewer, April 1937
23. Modern Brewer, April 1937
24. Article, Memphis Commercial Appeal, 7/3/1956
25. Interview with Doris Brigance Dolan. 7/30/2002
26. Interview with Jane Scott Howell, 11/3/2002
27. Interview with Jake Schorr, 12/11/2002
28. United States Beer Cans, Beer Can Collectors of America
29. Interview with Richard Campbell, 3/4/2003

Chapter 4

1. The Brewer's Digest, July 1940
2. Invoice from Wolff Printing Co., St. Louis, 11/20/1944
3. Invoice from Lawson-Getz Sporting Goods, Memphis, 9/23/1942
4. Invoice from Russwood Park, Memphis, 5/1/1945
5. Invoices from brewery to P.O.W. Camps, 11/30/1945
6. Letter to brewery from Stratton-Warren Hardware Co., Memphis, 9/27/1943
7. Various contracts between 11/6/1944 and 6/14/1945
8. Corporate income tax return for 1948

Chapter 5

1. Letter to brewery from Geo. Meyer Manf. Co., Cudahy, Wis., 4/15/1946
2. Invoice from Yellow Cab Co., 12/12/1943
3. Letter from brewery to Yellow Cab Co., 5/9/1946
4. Invoice from Merrill-Kremer Advertising, Memphis, to brewery, 8/12/1948
5. Letter from Grace Sign Co., St. Louis, 8/26/1946
6. Memo to all branch managers, 3/1/1948
7. Letter from brewery to Grace Sign Co., St. Louis, 8/26/1946
8. Memo to branch managers, 2/2/1947
9. Letter from Aidman Bottler's Supply Co., Brooklyn, N.Y., 5/29/1945
10. Order letter from brewery to Gaylord Container Corp., St. Louis, 8/16/1946
11. Memo from brewery to Helena, Ark. branch, 10/14/1946

Chapter 6

1. Corporate income tax return for 1951
2. Corporate income tax return for 1949
3. Interview with Ed Bretherick, 9/18/2002
4. Invoice from Balton Sign Co., Memphis, 2/27/1948
5. Invoice from Bradley Sign Co., Memphis, 9/30/1948
6. Memo to Paris, Tenn. branch, 7/10/1947
7. Memo to Shelbyville, Tenn. branch, 4/26/1947
8. Invoice from Grace Sign & Mfg., St Louis, 1/31/1947
9. Letter from Grace Sign Co., St. Louis, 12/6/1946
10. Invoice from Byrd Plastic Arts, Memphis, 12/30/1947
11. Invoices from Burk & Co. Sporting Goods, Nashville, Tenn., dated between 8/19/1947 and 6/12/1948 and invoice from Southern Uniform, Memphis, 7/7/1948
12. Invoices from baseball parks in Jackson, Tenn., Helena, Ark. & Clarksdale, Miss. for outfield fence ads dated between 5/12/1947 and 10/26/1948.
13. Memo to branches, 1/10/1947
14. Invoice from Lawson-Getz Sporting Goods, Memphis, 6/14/1948
15. Letter from brewery to Social Security Board, 5/16/1949
16. Interview with Jack Borg, 12/10/2002
17. Telegram from brewery to the Weiller Co., Philadelphia, Penn., 5/6/1948
18. Memo to Vincent Distributing Co., Little Rock, 4/20/1948
20. Invoice from Merrill-Kremer Advertising, Memphis, 9/30/1948
21. Memo from E.E. Dettwiller to city route salesmen, 8/14/1948
22. Invoice from Advertiser's Novelty Co., Memphis, 7/19/1948
23. Order confirmation letter to brewery from Dwinell Co., Kansas City, Mo., 12/13/1948
24. Telegram from Ernest Lee of Merrill-Kremer Advertising, Memphis, to brewery, 5/14/1948
25. Letter from Jacob B. Schorr to Walter Haas, Jackson Brewing Co., New Orleans, La. 4/12/1948
26. Liability policy, 1/1/1951
27. Tax report to State of Tennessee, 7/28/1949
28. Memo to all distributors about 5/22/1949 meeting, 5/16/1949
29. Various memos and letters to distributors, 1949
30. Order confirmation letter from Gamse Litho. Co., Baltimore, 2/3/1949
31. Invoice from Lewis Sign Co., Memphis, 4/29/1949
32. Interview with Jake Schorr, 12/11/2002
33. Interview with Fred Dettwiller, 3/1/2002
34. Interview with Jake Schorr, 12/11/2002
35. Interview with Ruth Conerly Meredith, 6/20/2002
36. Interview with Doris Brigance Dolan, 7/30/2002
37. Interview with Ruth Conerly Meredith, 6/20/2002

38. Interview with Bill Carter, 4/9/2002
39. Interview with Richard Campbell, 3/4/2002
40. Interview with Hal Newburger, 12/10/2002
41. Interview with Walter Crews, 6/20/2002
42. Interview with Katherine Kuehn, 4/10/2002
43. Interview with Joe Signaigo, 5/8/2002

Chapter 7

1. Interview with Buddy Krausnick, 1/20/2002
2. Letter from E.C. Krausnick, Jr. to WMCT-TV, 1/7/1949
3. Letter from J.B.Schorr to stockholders, 3/2/1951
4. Memo to branches in Arkansas, 8/10/1949
5. Invoices from sign companies (Lewis Signs, Memphis, McDaniel Signs, Greenwood, Miss., Cooper & Co., Jackson, Tenn. and Balton & Sons, Memphis) dated between 4/2/1949 and 9/1/1949 and memo from the brewery to Nashville, Tenn. branch, 6/30/1949
6. Interview with Buddy Krausnick, 1/20/2002
7. Interview with Jane Scott Howell, 11/3/2002

Chapter 8

1. Official notification letter to banks, 5/25/1950 and article, Memphis Commercial Appeal, 8/30/1952
2. Letter from E.E. Dettwiller to Jacob B. Schorr, 7/31/1951
3. Interview with Fred Dettwiller, 3/1/2002
4. Letter from brewery to U.S. Alcohol & Tobacco Tax Division, 1/3/1952 and article, Commercial Appeal, 8/30/1952
5. Stockholder filing with U.S. Alcohol and Tobacco Tax Division, 5/1/1952
6. Minutes of corporate board meeting, 8/13/1952
7. Minutes of corporate board meeting, 8/25/1952
8. Minutes of corporate board meeting, 8/15/1953
9. Modern Brewery Age, Sept. 1953
10. Interview with Bill Carter, 4/9/2002
11. Interview with Fred Dettwiller, 3/1/2002
12. Corporate income tax return for 1953
13. Numerous memos, letters and invoices dated between May and September, 1951
14. Letter from E.E. Dettwiller to Dyersburg, Tenn. branch, 4/3/51
15. Order confirmation letter from Grace Sign Co., St. Louis, 6/8/51
16. Interview with Bill Carter, 4/9/2002
17. Letter from brewery to stockholders, 6/23/52
18. Brewery advertising budget for 1952, submitted 1/28/52
19. Invoice from Westheimer & Block Advertising, St. Louis, 6/6/52
20. Script from company sales meeting, 3/9/52

21. Letter from brewery to Standard-Knapp Corp., 7/24/53
22. Interview with Buddy Krausnick, 6/19/2002
23. Memo from brewery to Wallerstein Labs, 1/29/52
24. Contract between Glazer Wholesale Drug Co. and brewery, 1/30/54
25. Shipping records between April and September 1954

Chapter 9

1. Interview with Ed Bretherick, 9/18/2002
2. Interview with Jim Reardon, 1/20/2002
3. Interview with Ed Bretherick, 9/18/2002
4. Interview with Bill Carter, 4/9/2002
5. Interview with Richard Campbell, 3/4/2003
6. Interview with Buddy Krausnick, 6/19/2002
7. Tax report to State of Tennessee, 12/31/1953
8. Interview with Buddy Krausnick, 3/13/2002
9. Letter from brewery to all employees, 9/10/1954
10. Interview with Joe Signaigo, 5/8/2002
11. Interview with Charlotte Clark, 4/10/2002
12. Interview with Doris Brigance Dolan, 7/30/2002
13. Letter from brewery to I.R.S., 1/25/1955
14. Interview with Doris Brigance Dolan, 7/30/2002
15. Interview with Buddy Krausnick, 3/13/2002
16. Order confirmation letters from brewery, 1/24/1956
17. Interview with Buddy Krausnick, 2/18/2002
18. Contract between brewery and Atlantic Brewing Co., Chicago, Ill., 12/31/1954
19. Contract between brewery and James A. Martin, 6/24/1955
20. Contract between brewery and Karchmer & Son, Memphis, 9/13/1955
21. Interview with Hal Newburger, 12/10/2002
22. Interview with Hal Newburger, 12/10/2002
23. Contract between brewery and Mr. Max Pinkerton/Mr. Mark Townsend, 1/20/1956
24. Form 27-C, U.S. Treasury Dept, I.R.S., filed 4/1/1956
25. Interview with Buddy Krausnick, 1/20/2002

TENNESSEE BREWING COMPANY
BARRELS SOLD/CORPORATE PROFITS (LOSS)

Year	Barrels Sold	Corporate Profit (Loss)
1885	Not available	Not available
1886	Not available	Not available
1887	Not available	Not available
1888	Not available	Not available
1889	Not available	Not available
1890	Not available	Not available
1891	Not available	Not available
1892	36,132	Not available
1893	Not available	Not available
1894	Not available	Not available
1895	Not available	Not available
1896	Not available	Not available
1897	Not available	Not available
1898	Not available	Not available
1899	Not available	Not available
1900	45,929	Not available
1901	Not available	Not available
1902	Not available	Not available
1903	Not available	Not available
1904	Not available	Not available
1905	Not available	Not available
1906	Not available	Not available
1907	Not available	Not available
1908	80,149	Not available
1909	73,910	Not available
1910	79,148	Not available
1911	84,093	Not available
1912	85,477	Not available
1913	90,657	Not available
1914	30,397	Not available
1915	5317	Not available

Prohibition

113

Year	Barrels Sold	Corporate Profit (Loss)
1933	—	(7322.12)
1934	27,059	(6886.47)
1935	34,711	(24,496.24)
1936	41,080	8,008.64
1937	47,760	4208.32
1938	46,566	(8678.97)
1939	53,864	19,291.08
1940	77,789	72,245.42
1941	120,606	125,692.62
1942	150,171	97,649.25
1943	146,228	97,505.15
1944	144,133	55,682.35
1945	153,318	71,049.03
1946	142,988	190,492.25
1947	208,098	528,123.24
1948	208,612	382,678.92
1949	175,134	223,536.79
1950	137,935	115,875.13
1951	110,256	(37,768.02)
1952	87,124	(145,329.34)
1953	67,410	(291,457.51)
1954	51,498	(493,316.33)
1955	0	(234,341,17)

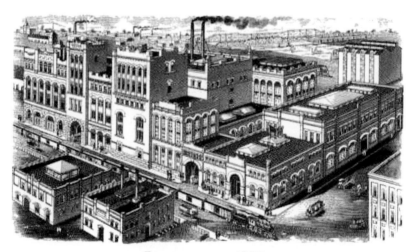

ESTABLISHED 1885

TENNESSEE BREWING COMPANY
OFFICERS

President

John W. Schorr	1885-1917
Jacob B. Schorr, Sr.	1935-1952
Charles C. Starnes	1952-1953
E. C. Krausnick, Jr.	1953-1954

Vice President

Peter Saussenthaler	1885-1899
Caspar Koehler *	1899-1910
Leo Rassieur **	1899-1912
Julius Koehler *	1910-1912, 1933-1935
Julius Koehler	1912-1917
Fred Uhrig **	1933-1935
E. C. Krausnick, Sr.	1935-1951
E. C. Krausnick, Sr. ***	1951-1952
Edgar E. Dettwiller****	1951
Charles C. Starnes	1952
E.C. Krausnick, Jr.	1952-1953
J.B. Schorr, Jr. *****	1953-1954
B. Frank Jenkins ****	1954

Treasurer

Caspar Koehler	1885-1898
Jacob B. Schorr, Sr.	1898-1905, 1917
John W. Schorr	1905-1917
unknown	1935-1938
A. E. Kammerer	1938-1939
E. C. Krausnick, Sr.	1940-1952
Charles C. Starnes	1952-1953
W. C. McWillie	1953-1954

Secretary

Caspar Koehler	1885-1890
Adam J. Uhrig	1891-1899
Jacob B. Schorr, Jr.	1899-1917
E. C. Krausnick, Sr.	1934-1937
John S. Reardon	1937-1950
Charles C. Starnes	1950-1952
E. C. Krausnick, Jr.	1952-1953
J. B. Schorr, Jr.	1954

*	1st VP	****	VP/Sales
**	2nd VP	*****	VP/Production
***	VP/Finance		